HIGH-IMPACT
PUBLIC
SPEAKING
FOR
BUSINESS
AND THE
PROFESSIONS

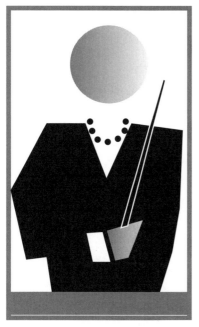

J. REGIS O'CONNOR
Western Kentucky University

Printed on recyclable paper

NTC Publishing Group
Lincolnwood, Illinois USA

Acknowledgments

page 144: from *The Nobel Prize Lecture*. New York: Phelps-Stokes Fund, 1986.
page 150: from *The Nobel Prize Lecture*. New York: Phelps-Stokes Fund, 1986.
page 154: from *School Administrator's Public Speaking Portfolio with Model Speeches and Anecdotes*, P. Susan Mamchak and Steven R. Mamchak. West Nyak, NJ: Parker, 1983.
page163: from *I Gotta Tell You*, Lee A. Iacocca. Detroit: Wayne State University Press, 1994.

Every effort has been made to contact copyright holders. The publishers will be glad to rectify any omissions or errors upon notification.

Editor: Marisa L. L'Heureux
Development: Elizabeth S. MacDonell, Write One Consulting
Cover and interior design and art: Ophelia M. Chambliss
Production Manager: Rosemary Dolinski

Library of Congress Cataloging-in-Publication Data

O'Connor, J. Regis
    High-impact public speaking for business and the professions / J. Regis O'Connor.
        p.   cm.
    Includes index.
    ISBN 0-8442-3413-3. — ISBN 0-8442-3414-1 (pbk.)
    1. Business communication.   2. Public speaking.   I. Title.
HF5718.O33   1996
808.5'1—dc20   96-13430
                                                              CIP

ontents

Chapter Two

SPEECH PREPARATION:

Chapter Three

CHOOSING EFFECTIVE LANGUAGE:

Chapter Four

DELIVERING THE SPEECH:
Using Your Body and Your Voice

CHAPTER FIVE

SPEAKING TO INFORM   79

CHAPTER SIX

SPEAKING TO MOTIVATE AND PERSUADE

Chapter Seven

SPECIAL KINDS OF SPEAKING

Appendix

MODEL SPEECHES

Preface

Communication overwhelmingly pervades today's business environment. Indeed, many management theorists would claim communication as *the* essential function by which managers at any level of a company live their corporate lives. Whether you are owner-manager of a mom-and-pop shop, department head for a midsized industrial plant, or CEO of an international conglomerate, your primary tools for assuring your company's survival and success are the spoken and written word. Your skill as a communicator assuredly affects your employees' productivity, your clients' and customers' loyalty, your credibility as a manager, and your organization's bottom line. Communication in corporate America takes multiple forms, including job interviews, performance appraisal reviews, conference calls, meetings, memoranda, letters, reports, policy statements, workshops, and direct sales.

The regular use of the public speech, however, has often been overlooked by companies as a major power tool with which to drive a business. This widespread neglect of public speaking as advertiser, promoter, motivator, and persuader surely accounts for billions of dollars of neglected opportunity each year in the United States alone.

Why have organizations not seized the potential of the public speech? One answer is that many otherwise solid communicators in this country are *afraid to give public speeches.* In repeated surveys, the American people, when asked to rank situations they fear the most, have listed the fear of speaking in public as their worst dread. Managers and executives who boldly risk millions of dollars or lay-off a third of their workforce turn into quivering gelatin when invited to address an audience, despite their evident expertise on the topic. Many that *do* muster the courage to ascend the platform find themselves debilitated by a sometimes paralyzing stage fright that ruins their speech and drains them of any daring to try again. But for those who succeed in conquering the fear, the rewards can prove career-changing. In his autobiography, Lee Iacocca, former chairperson of Chrysler, confessed his early fear of speechmaking and described how he vowed to overcome his handicap; eventually he became a compelling crusader for Chrysler on the national scene. Many may not experience such a dazzling reversal of oratorical prowess, of course, but the benefits in terms of heightened self-confidence and improved business can prove sizable. Any opportunity for a reasonably effective public speaker to inform and influence groups of listeners about one's business can generate greater success.

A second reason for neglect of the public speech may lie in the difficulty of producing a truly effective public presentation. Public speaking requires a great deal of detailed preparation—homework to which some speakers may be unable or unwilling to commit. But more importantly, many managers and executives lack the training to craft a dynamic and convincing speech. A speech is not simply making a few pertinent remarks—that is not nearly the same thing as a thoroughly developed message, designed for a specific audience and fully supported by sound thought and solid evidence. Great public speeches are embarrassingly rare on our national scene nowadays, and perhaps nowhere more strikingly so than in our business community. John Widgodsky, Executive Vice-President of Fruit-of-the-Loom, Inc., believes that the public speech is underutilized in today's business environment, sometimes because the executive's credibility has already been damaged by earlier bungled attempts. But it doesn't have to be so.

Your power as a public speaker will flow first from your success in controlling stage fright and then from exhaustive preparation and confident presentation. *High-Impact Public Speaking for Business and the Professions* begins by directly confronting the widespread problem of speech apprehension—its causes, its symptoms, *and* its benefits. Once a public speaker learns to harness the fear, stage fright actually becomes an ally, enlivening a speech and empowering a speaker in a way that previously seemed unattainable.

Chapter 2 then presents a complete outline of each step of the speech preparation process, beginning with audience analysis and culminating with the final rehearsal session. Neglecting thoroughgoing preparation here would be like a builder starting construction without a blueprint—a catastrophe waiting to happen.

Chapter 3 focuses on choosing effective language, probably *the* single element in speechmaking that separates the good speech from the great speech. Understanding differences between written and spoken language, creating levels of emphasis, and using figurative language are several of the language tools that give force and dynamism to a speech.

Chapter 4 covers speech delivery. Several methods for presenting speeches are compared, with the extemporaneous method highlighted as the most successful for most, though not all, presentations. A number of both verbal and nonverbal delivery skills are presented.

The final three chapters delve into speechmaking with various goals or purposes. Chapter 5 deals with speaking to inform and describes compelling speech openers, how to psychologically close your speech, methods for adroitly conducting a question-and-answer period, and the effective use of visual aids.

Chapter 6 delves into speeches to motivate and persuade—ways by which to actualize your employees and sell your company. This involves discovering the specific needs of a given set of listeners (that is, what does my audience want from my speech?), establishing your prestige as a speaker on your topic, and being reasonable and responsible as a persuader.

Chapter 7 presents a number of special kinds of speeches focusing on people and special occasions. These include speeches of introduction, speeches of presentation, testimonial speeches, and dedication speeches—those speeches that generally celebrate your people and your organization.

The book concludes with an appendix of ten model speeches of various types.

Though the primary audience for this book is the business executive at any level of management, would-be public speakers outside corporate life can hone their speaking skills for a wide array of purposes. Leaders of nonprofit organizations, attorneys, consultants, legislators, owners of small businesses, members of town councils—all can markedly improve their effectiveness through a detailed study of the art and science of public speaking. For that matter, any thinking person wishing to influence groups of friends or neighbors about local issues can have notable impact through the power of the public speech.

J. Regis O'Connor

CHAPTER ONE

Stage Fright: Harnessing the Fear

The human brain is a wonderful thing. It starts working the moment you are born and never stops until you stand up to speak in public.

This quote from well-known entertainer George Jessel illustrates what is probably the most common problem faced by those who give public speeches—the problem of stage fright. This age-old scourge of public speakers may begin to bother you even now as you read these opening paragraphs, but you should take heart in the realization that you *can* conquer the fear if you really want to, and can actually make your stage fright work for you.

For the speaker who has never learned to overcome it, stage fright can be a huge obstacle that can make the difference between your success and failure as a speaker. In this chapter, you will face stage fright head on. You will explore its causes, see what effects it can have (good as well as bad), and learn methods for controlling it. Once you can view stage fright as a normal part of the public-speaking experience, you are ready to begin building the kind of confidence you need to be an effective speaker.

Of course you may be one of those people who does not experience stage fright. Some speakers feel as relaxed in front of an audience as they do chatting with a few friends around the dinner table. If that is your happy circumstance, be glad about it, but do not get overconfident—being free of stage fright by no means guarantees that you are a better speaker than someone who suffers from it. It seems, however, according to self-reports from numerous speakers, that the majority of us *do* fear public speaking, thus making it a "misery loves company" experience if nothing else. In other words, if you have been feeling that you are one of the very few who gets sweaty palms and a queasy stomach at the very thought of giving a speech, you couldn't be more wrong. Research figures show that over half of inexperienced speakers surveyed reported stage fright, and very few experienced speakers were totally free of nervousness.

CONTROLLING STAGE FRIGHT

Although the term *stage fright* is often reserved for public speakers and actors, these same symptoms are also common among tennis and baseball players, concert pianists, and humorists—in other words, most people who give a public performance of some kind. Nor are these uneasy feelings reserved for inexperienced speakers and performers. Many famous people seasoned in appearing before the public have reported stage fright. Even Sir Winston Churchill, considered one of the most influential speakers of the twentieth century, once confessed that he endured stage fright when delivering his speeches. The major difference in the effect stage fright has on a beginner and on an experienced speaker comes from how each handles the nervousness once it occurs. Although there is no substitute for experience when learning to control stage fright, speakers can begin to build confidence with their first speech, if they begin correctly.

Understanding Why Stage Fright Occurs

The first step in building speaker confidence lies in understanding why you usually feel nervous when speaking in front of a group (or, for some people, even while *preparing* to speak in public). Stage fright often affects people in physical ways—sweaty palms, queasy stomach, dry mouth, excessive perspiration, increased heart rate, shortness of breath. But the true beginnings of stage fright are mental, not physical. When preparing to present a speech, a strong psychological tension can build within you, a tension that comes from two conflicting realizations: (1) I desperately want to perform well and make a good impression, and (2) I may not be very successful. Your realization that all eyes will be focused upon you and that you will be the center of attention intensifies your desire for success and your fear of failure and embarrassment. Most people find it difficult, if not impossible, to take a nonchalant, "so what" attitude about the outcome of speeches they are about to give.

If you have ever been called upon to sing a solo, play an instrument, or perform as an athlete in front of a crowd, you probably can recall having felt some of the symptoms of stage fright, such as queasy stomach and sweaty palms. A teammate of basketball legend Bill Russell once noted, "Bill has left his lunch in men's rooms all over this country." Before a big game, Russell literally got sick at the prospect of performing, but once the game began, he was able to channel all of that nervous energy into fantastic basketball. How did he do it? By learning to control his fear and making it work *for* him rather than against him.

Viewing Controlled Stage Fright as Helpful

You can learn to control your stage fright in much the same way as Bill Russell—by recognizing that you can channel that nervousness and inner tension and make it an asset for your speech or presentation rather than a liability. Such inner tension causes your muscles to tighten, your heart and breathing rates to increase, and more adrenaline and oxygen to pump through your body. The result is that your brain and muscles become "supercharged," priming you for your upcoming performance. In effect, your body carries out its natural function of preparing you to meet a special situation.

Well-known speakers have reported that their most successful speeches have been those they were most nervous about beforehand. For instance, Lee Iacocca has said, "Fear takes a lot of energy, I discovered, and channeling all that energy into the speech itself is the best way to make it work *for* you instead of *against* you." On other occasions, when such speakers were less concerned about making a good impression or felt overconfident, their presentations sometimes fell flat. The simple realization that stage fright is natural prior to a speech—and actually an aid to sharper thinking—can itself be a means of controlling it. Controlled stage fright, then, can aid you in becoming a better speaker.

Avoiding Uncontrolled Stage Fright

Inexperienced speakers, unused to feeling the symptoms of stage fright, often think that their dry throat or sweaty palms spell certain doom for their speech. The greater these feelings become, the more intense the stage fright symptoms become. This in turn leads to more worry, which leads to worse symptoms, and so on, and so on. The result is uncontrolled, or "runaway," stage fright. Its effects are quite different than controlled stage fright and may ruin a well-prepared speech.

Runaway stage fright takes one of two forms. The first is borne of lack of confidence and usually strikes before the speech begins. Many times the speaker who experiences this form of runaway stage fright is actually well prepared for the speech but has allowed the symptoms of stage fright to snowball. As a result, the speaker's self-confidence is at a low point by the time the speech begins—the very moment he or she needs it the most. The second form arises from poor preparation combined with overconfidence and ordinarily does not occur until after the speech has begun. When it occurs, this second kind of runaway stage fright strikes suddenly and takes the speaker by surprise. Inadequate preparation does not always surface during introductory remarks, but it may become obvious once the speaker has reached the body of the speech. At that point, a moment of forgetfulness is all that is needed to trigger sudden runaway stage fright.

Since both too little confidence and overconfidence can initiate stage fright, the wise speaker must aim for that critical middle ground—a degree of self-assurance that comes from thorough preparation, tempered with a realization of the unpredictable nature of the public speaking situation.

Remembering that Stage Fright Feels Worse Than It Looks

Stage fright is much more noticeable to the speaker than to the audience. Beginning speakers sometimes experience the feelings caused by stage fright so intensely that they fail to realize that their listeners aren't nearly so aware of their nervousness. Your listeners can't see or hear your tightening stomach muscles, for instance, nor will they ordinarily notice your sweaty palms or dry mouth. They might notice a slight tremor in your voice occasionally or a faster-than-normal breathing rate, but even these symptoms bother the speaker much more than the listeners. Realizing this fact can make a big difference for some stage-fright sufferers.

Chronic victims of stage fright are generally not content to worry only about their possible inability to speak clearly or remember ideas. Some like to worry in big bundles, so they also get concerned about what kind of impression their stage-fright symptoms are making on the audience. For such giant-economy-size worriers, it should be comforting to realize that stage fright always feels much worse than it appears to others. Unless you foolishly call specific attention to your stage fright with comments such as, "I'm so nervous, I'm not sure this speech is making sense," your listeners will often be unaware that you are nervous, let alone frightened.

CONTROLLING YOUR NERVOUSNESS

Before you began reading this chapter, you very likely imagined that the best way to deal with stage fright was to rid yourself of it entirely. But by now you know that a limited amount of stage fright can actually be helpful. The trick, then, is learning to control that limited amount. There are a number of ways you can do this, including preparing thoroughly, relaxing before you speak, concentrating on your audience, and using nonverbal movements and gestures, to name a few.

Preparing Thoroughly

One effective method for controlling stage fright is to prepare thoroughly for each public speech. Since most stage fright comes from a fear of not succeeding in front of an audience, thorough preparation beforehand can guarantee that about 90 percent of your speech will go smoothly. Since you are the speaker, you are the person with the greatest control over what occurs during your speech. You can make certain you are well prepared by heeding the following four steps, each of which we will discuss in more detail in Chapter 2:

1. Study your topic.

2. Analyze the needs of your audience.

3. Research and outline the ideas of your speech.

4. Rehearse your presentation sufficiently.

Once you have completed these steps, you will have little reason to fear that something unplanned or unpleasant will happen. You can begin your speech with confidence.

Of course the possibility always exists that something unexpected might occur (a loud noise, a heckler, a fire drill), but such interruptions happen very seldom. Still, knowing that such distractions *can* occasionally arise will keep you sufficiently alert, yet not allow you to become overconfident.

Thorough preparation not only gives you the right level of confidence before your speech begins, it also supports you once you have begun speaking. One of the greatest fears of most new speakers is the fear of forgetting part of their speech. After you have gained some experience giving speeches, you will realize that this is not such a serious problem as it may first seem. For one thing, your audience ordinarily does not know in advance what you intend to say, so even if you leave out a large section of your planned presentation, no one is the wiser. (Incidentally, don't call attention to an omission by mentioning you have forgotten something or by appearing confused.) Second, most speakers have notes available during their speeches to help jog their memories should they forget a point. Finally, forgetting is seldom a problem if a speaker has rehearsed thoroughly and correctly. You will see in the next chapter that correct preparation does not mean word-for-word memorization of your speech. If you try doing this, you put a tremendous burden on your memory, and, as a result, you *are* likely to forget.

Relaxing before You Speak

Even when thoroughly prepared, many speakers experience physical tension shortly before they are scheduled to speak. Some can feel their neck muscles tightening. Others feel mild stomach upset. Many notice more rapid heart and breathing rates. Although these are symptoms rather than causes of stage fright, speakers quite frequently find it helpful to relax physically before beginning their speech. Relaxing your body is a way of convincing yourself that things aren't hopeless.

The relaxation techniques listed below can help you reduce some of the physical symptoms of stage fright. These should be exercised as close to the start of your speech as possible, without being noticeable to your audience. Most of these techniques can be done privately just before you join your listeners:.

- Force yourself to yawn widely several times. Fill your lungs with air each time by breathing deeply.
- Let your head hang down as far as possible on your chest for several moments. Then slowly rotate your head in a full circle, at the same time allowing your eyelids to droop lazily. Let your mouth and lower jaw hang open loosely. Repeat this rolling motion very slowly five or six times.
- Sit in a slumped position in a chair as if your were a rag doll. Allow your arms to dangle beside the chair, your head to slump on your chest, and your mouth to hang open. Then tighten all the muscles in your body one at a time, starting with your toes and working up to your neck. Next, gradually relax each set of muscles, starting at the top and working back down to your toes. Repeat this process several times.

Realizing that Audiences Tend to Be Sympathetic

Audiences are usually sympathetic to the problem of stage fright. Most listeners realize that they could have the same feelings if they were in your shoes, and they show by their treatment of the speaker that they would expect the same treatment in return. Audiences want to see speakers succeed, not fail. To the extent that listeners may notice symptoms of stage fright, they will usually react in a friendly and encouraging fashion.

Developing the Right Attitude

If you are like most speakers, you are destined to feel some of the symptoms of stage fright before every speech. Since it is nearly impossible to prevent the symptoms of stage fright from occurring, the key to success lies in your mental attitude toward your feelings. Once the butterflies-in-the-stomach and the shaking knees begin, train yourself to think in the following sequence:

1. Since the time for my speech is getting near, what I'm feeling are symptoms of stage fright.
2. This is my body's way of preparing me to meet the speech situation.
3. Once my speech begins, this tension will serve to sharpen my thinking and give vitality to my presentation.

This thought process is what one speech writer called "training the butterflies to fly in formation," an attitude that focuses the speaker on the opportunity stage fright provides: harnessing your tension and making it work *for* you. Once you begin to recognize stage fright as your ally rather than your enemy, your runaway nervousness fades rapidly, a controlled level of apprehension takes over, and your speechmaking begins to show marked improvement.

Concentrating on Your Topic

Many speakers lack confidence because they are thinking too much about themselves. They may ask themselves beforehand, "Will I do as well as that last speaker when my turn comes?" Then during the presentation it might be, "Should I be making more gestures?" Or, "I don't think I'm doing very well with my speech so far!" Instead of critiquing yourself, work at developing a strong enthusiasm for your topic. Say to yourself, "I have a topic that I want to share with these listeners. I want to make certain they are well informed (or persuaded), and I will do everything in my power to ensure that they are." Once you begin thinking in these terms, the worst symptoms of stage fright are likely to fade into the background.

But you have to work at developing a confident attitude about your subject matter. Don't get up in front of an audience with the feeling, "I *have* to give a presentation today." Instead, think exhilarating thoughts like, "I have a *presentation* to give today!"

Concentrating on Your Audience

While you are delivering your speech, search the faces of your audience to make certain they are following your ideas and to see whether the listeners agree with those ideas. If you perceive boredom growing among your audience, change tactics and attempt to regain their attention and interest. Of course in any audience some listeners will appear more interested than others. When this occurs, it is perfectly all right to give more of your attention to the interested listeners. Their obvious appreciation for your speech can be a great confidence-builder for you.

Some speakers make the mistake of attempting to interest the most bored or even disgusted-looking member of the audience. Nearly every audience will have several such people. If you change your approach to suit them, you may be ruining what was a highly rewarding speech for 90 percent of your listeners. Only when a sizable portion of your audience is showing signs of boredom or disinterest should you begin changing your tactics. We'll talk more about different types of audiences in Chapter 6.

If you concentrate on looking for audience feedback and making appropriate responses to it, you will have little time to think about yourself. As you think less about yourself, your stage fright will be controlled and your confidence will increase.

Injecting a Little Humor

Humor has long been used as a means of reducing tension between speaker and audience. Getting a laugh from an audience builds confidence rapidly, because it assures you that there is little to fear from the listeners. Once your speech has begun, injecting a bit of humor—particularly near the beginning—relaxes you more effectively than anything else. If not overdone, humor relaxes your audience members as well. When using humor, observe these precautions:

- Prepare humor thoroughly beforehand, making certain it will be understood and appreciated by this particular audience. A joke that falls flat can destroy a speaker's confidence rather than build it.

- Use humor mainly during the speech introduction, sprinkling lesser amounts throughout the remainder of the speech.

- Do not overuse humor.
- Avoid offensive jokes.

We'll discuss the use of humor in greater detail in Chapter 5.

Using Nonverbal Movements and Gestures

Have you ever narrowly missed being in a car accident? If so, you probably noticed that right after your near miss you were trembling. Your body was getting rid of the tension that had built up suddenly when you saw the accident coming. In much the same way, moving your body while speaking helps dissipate some of the tension you may feel and can also help relieve other symptoms of stage fright.

Needless to say, any movements you make should be suited to the speech and the audience. All kinds of movement will reduce tension, but some forms look pretty ridiculous during a public speech or presentation. Inexperienced speakers, in a subconscious attempt to reduce stage fright, occasionally use movements that tend to distract the listeners from the message. Among these awkward movements, several have become fairly common. The Ping-Pong Pacers, for instance, constantly pace to and fro in front of the audience until the listeners appear to be viewing a ping-pong match. The Lectern Leeches grab the sides of the lectern so tightly their knuckles turn white. The Hair-Tossers, whose hair may not always be in their eyes, regularly toss their heads to get it out of the way anyway. The Pencil-Twirlers manage to draw all their audience's attention to a pencil, paper clip, rubber band, or note card they are folding, spindling, or mutilating as they speak.

Movements that help communicate your message nonverbally are the only kind you should strive to make while speaking. Such movements release nervous tension just as effectively as the distracting ones, but have the added advantage of helping you get your message across. Such movements fall into three broad categories, each of which we will discuss in detail in Chapter 4.

EYE CONTACT. Remember that your eyes may be your most effective means of body-motion communication. Beginning speakers often struggle with the question, "Must I look right into the eyes of my listeners?" Eye contact is very desirable because it gives each audience member the feeling that you are speaking to him or her personally. However, if you find in your first few speeches that you get less confused and nervous by simply looking at your audience as a whole and not directly into individuals' eyes, then do so. Once you have had some practice and have gained a bit of confidence on the platform, begin to look directly into the eyes of a number of your listeners.

GESTURES. Although some people tend to "talk with their hands" more than others do, most beginning public speakers tend to be too "quiet" with their arms and hands. Practicing specific gestures for a particular point in a speech is not wise. Gestures during a live performance should not look practiced; they should look and *be* natural. One way to achieve this is to use general arm and hand movements during rehearsal. This is likely to loosen you up and lead to similar natural arm and hand gestures during the speech.

Gestures also include movements of the head and face. While speaking, try to move your head frequently to look from one part of your audience to another. You should also vary your facial expression to correspond with the thought patterns of your speech. Again, your movements should be natural.

PLATFORM MOVEMENT. Except during very formal speeches, a speaker should occasionally change positions on the platform. Moving the entire body is called *platform movement*. Platform movement is especially appropriate when a speaker is making a major transition in thought patterns, when it is desirable to get closer to a section of your audience to show greater confidentiality or intimacy, or where attention seems to be flagging. Movement can also be useful in simply providing variety after a speaker has been in one position for some time. Naturally, any amount of total body movement that resembles the antics of a Ping-Pong Pacer is too much. Of course, in situations where a stationary microphone is necessary, no platform movement is possible.

Handling Specific Symptoms of Nervousness

Some symptoms of stage fright may bother you more than others. Exhibit 1.1 shows several of the more obvious ones, with suggestions for handling each. Successfully dealing with symptoms that you find particularly annoying will help you build your confidence.

Speaking as Often as You Can

Confidence in public speaking is built more by the experience of giving speeches and presentations than by anything else. If you genuinely want to feel at ease about public speaking, you need to volunteer or accept offers to speak before groups whenever your knowledge, experience, or involvement in a given topic can genuinely benefit your audience. Make a commitment to yourself to speak in public (or to a group) at least once a month. Where, you ask? Here are some ideas:

EXHIBIT 1.1   Stage Fright Symptoms and Solutions

Symptoms	Solutions
trembling hands and a rattling manuscript	Use 3" x 5" cards. Place them on the lectern and slide each card to one side after it has been used.
stumbling over words—getting "tongue twisted"	Deliberately slow down your speaking rate until the problem disappears.
the feeling that you cannot get enough breath	Speak slowly. Take longer pauses between sentences. Breathe from your diaphragm and through your nose.
unwillingness to look at the audience	In the beginning, do not look directly at individuals. Instead, look just above their heads or slightly to one side of their faces. Later, pick the friendliest face in the audience and look first at that person.
excessive perspiration	Ignore it. Do not call attention to it by wiping you hands or forehead.
cold hands and feet	Make some platform movement and gestures.
hoarse or squeaky voice	Before a speech, tape record your rehearsal sessions and concentrate on eliminating vocal problems. If this problem occurs during a speech, ignore it.
dry mouth	Speak slowly to avoid getting tongue tied. Do not lick your lips in front of the audience.
tense muscles	Use platform movements and gestures.
cramps, butterflies in stomach	Remember that the audience is ordinarily not aware of such symptoms. Ignore them as much as possible.
wanting to return to your seat	Resist this feeling at all costs. The best way to control stage fright is by having experience in public speaking.
feeling inferior	Try dressing for the speech in the outfit that makes you look your best. Naturally, it must be appropriate to the audience and occasion.

- Volunteer to give a presentation within your work group or to upper management.
- If you *are* upper management, speak to your employees.
- Talk about your company at local service clubs. Make sales presentations to customers.
- Join Toastmasters.
- Participate as a speaker or discussant in your professional organization's annual conferences.
- Volunteer for the speakers' bureaus of nonprofit organizations.

The bottom line is this: If you have an important message to share with a set of listeners, you need not be an orator to succeed. Your enthusiasm about your topic and your willingness to inform or persuade your audience will be appreciated, whether or not the mechanics of your speech are carried out with textbook precision. Audiences are extraordinarily tolerant of public speakers, if for no other reason than most listeners know they would be just as nervous if they were the ones standing in front of the group. If you seriously wish to control your stage fright and become a better speaker, you have to give a number of speeches.

CHAPTER TWO

*S*peech Preparation: Choosing the Best Blueprint

*I*n order to construct a solid and functional house, builders must start with a set of plans. The process of drawing up the plans is, in some ways, as important as the actual construction process itself. Many critical questions must be answered in the plans, such as, "Will the foundation be adequate to support the weight of the house? Are the rooms arranged properly for maximum convenience? Is the structure placed in the best possible position on the lot?"

By first building the house in their minds and on paper, builders can save great amounts of time and money. A mistake at this early stage is easily fixed; mistakes made after construction has started, on the other hand, are generally very costly to correct.

Wise speakers build their speeches in much the same manner as builders construct houses—first in their minds and on paper. Each speaker's preparation, like the builder's, should answer many critical questions: What topic fits the occasion and will be of interest to my audience? What strategy best suits the particular audience I will be addressing? Where can I locate the best sources of information and supporting evidence? In what order should I present my ideas? Without ample time to answer these questions beforehand, a speaker runs a great risk of having the speech crumble into a disorganized jumble of words. Conversely, a well-prepared speaker goes into a speech confident of the outcome. This chapter deals with the preparatory stages in giving a speech—those important steps taken well before the date of delivery will determine whether the presentation will prove smooth and natural or halting and awkward. The steps in the speech preparation process are illustrated in Exhibit 2.1.

DETERMINING YOUR GENERAL PURPOSE

The first part of speech preparation involves focusing on your topic and determining your general purpose for giving the speech or presentation in the first place. This process usually begins when you are asked (by invitation or mandate) to make a speech or presentation about some topic in which you have a certain level of knowledge or expertise. Once you have agreed to speak, determine your general purpose. Will you be informing your listeners? Persuading or convincing them? Does the situation call for a special kind of speech, such as an acceptance speech, or perhaps a speech whose purpose is simply to entertain your audience? Once you have determined your general purpose, you can begin to focus your topic by tailoring it to fit the particular interests of your listeners and by narrowing it to fit the time limit available to you.

As was mentioned in the introduction, the general purposes for which speeches are given fall into a fairly small number of categories. The three main categories of speeches are:

1. **Speeches to Inform.** Here your general purpose is to teach your listeners new information. In short, you want them to know more about your topic after your speech than they did beforehand.

2. **Speeches to Persuade.** Persuasive speeches are designed to intensify or change listeners' attitudes, beliefs, or behavior patterns.

Exhibit 2.1

The Speech Preparation Process

Determine Your General Purpose

↓

Analyze Your Audience

↓

Focus On Your Specific Purpose

↓

Research Your Topic

↓

Organize and Outline Your Speech

↓

Rehearse Your Speech

3. **Speeches to Entertain.** Speeches to entertain are given simply for the enjoyment and relaxation of the listeners. They are frequently delivered as after-dinner speeches.

In addition, speeches are given to demonstrate a product or process, motivate groups to perform and achieve, eulogize those who have died, say farewell when someone is moving or retiring, introduce a main speaker, present or accept an award or gift, dedicate buildings, keynote a conference or convention, and promote a positive image of an event or organization. By far, however, speeches to inform and persuade will dominate the business speaker's requests.

You can also give several different types of speeches on the same broad topic. In the morning, you may present a training program to new hires about how to sell your company's brand of clothing (informative speech), then in the afternoon find yourself selling the merits of your clothing company to a potential lender (persuasive speech). Same topic, different speech purpose. You may even find yourself informing and persuading within the same speech. In a product demonstration to a customer group, for instance, you might start by informing the customers of the product's capabilities, then later switch to a persuasive role as you try to convince them to buy the product. Additionally, you may make effective use of humor within informative or persuasive speeches, either to clarify or to sell your ideas or products.

Occasionally, you may not accept an invitation to give the speech at all—when you have the option. The usual reasons for such a refusal might be that you recognize you are not the informed "expert" on the topic that your inviter thought you were, you are not given sufficient preparation time before the date of the speech, or perhaps you don't have enough enthusiasm for the topic to make the speech occasion sufficiently worthwhile for your audience. Such reasons may certainly be valid on occasions, but typically requests for you to speak will not be issued unless you are known to have a solid message to present.

ANALYZING YOUR AUDIENCE

Not every subject that is interesting to you will automatically be of stirring interest to each member of your audience. By and large, however, persons interested in your topic (specifically or more generally) will typically form 80 to 90 percent of your audience. It is when you face an amalgamated audience—an audience composed of persons with widely divergent interests—that you have to plan ways of maintaining interest and even enthusiasm among all segments of your audience. However, with enough experience and enthusiasm for a topic, you should be able to make your speeches interesting to almost anyone. Begin by asking yourself, "How can I make this topic interesting and acceptable to all the members of my audience?" Answering this question involves audience analysis, one of the most important steps in speech preparation.

Audience analysis begins with a series of questions designed to probe the relationship between the needs of your intended audience and your own goals and purposes as a speaker. Ask yourself questions such as the following:

- Do my audience members already know much about this topic?
- What can I tell them about this topic that they do not already know?

- Will this topic interest some audience members more than others?
- If I take a stand on this issue, will my audience agree with me?
- If they do not agree, what interests or needs do they have through which I might change their minds?

Asking and answering questions such as these about your audience will help you organize your topic for presentation to a specific group of people. Just as in a one-to-one conversation, an audience tends to be responsive when members perceive that a speaker has taken their knowledge, interests, needs, and attitudes into consideration.

From a practical standpoint, your best opportunity to analyze your audience is not immediately before or during the speech but rather at the time you are asked to address a particular group. Typically, your boss, customer, lenders, conference chair, or the like will ask if you are willing to talk on some topic of interest to the audience. When you agree, be sure to ask your invitee (or be sure you already know) the answers to the following important questions:

- About how many persons will be in attendance? (The answer may dictate special needs, such as whether you will need a microphone.)
- What will be the gender composition of my audience? (Women and men may sometimes react differently to various topics.)
- If the speech purpose is to persuade or convince, what are my prospective listeners' attitudes about my topic? (For, against, apathetic, uninformed?)
- What about the age of my listeners? Will there be a mixture? (Younger listeners often see matters quite differently than older audience members.)
- What will be the level of formal education among my listeners? (This will sometimes dictate the level of language used.)
- Will my audience be a highly specialized one? (If so, you may use insider language common to that group.)

FOCUSING ON YOUR SPECIFIC PURPOSE

Once you have determined your general topic and analyzed your audience, you are ready to focus on the specific purpose for your speech. The specific purpose is precisely what you want your listeners to know, think, believe, or do as a result of hearing your speech. Therefore, the easiest way to focus in on your specific purpose is to write out a single declarative sentence in which you state as clearly as you can exactly what you want your listeners to know, believe, think, or do by the time your speech is over. This is called the *purpose sentence*. It will serve as the master guide by which you will write down all the details of your speech outline. Following are a few examples of purpose sentences. Notice that the first three examples focus on informative purposes while the latter three focus on persuasive purposes:

- My purpose is to inform our salesforce about which software products to recommend for use with our latest line of computers.
- My purpose is to inform my staff about using time management techniques in their daily work.
- My purpose is to present our current financial standing to stockholders at their annual meeting.
- My purpose is to urge our marketing department to use focus groups whenever possible.
- My purpose is to expand our use of videoconferencing as a cost containment practice vis-à-vis air travel.
- My purpose is to convince a potential client that my consulting services meet her needs and budget parameters.

As you develop your speech purpose, also keep in mind the time limit available for the presentation. Some topics may be too broad for a brief speech and will need to be pared down; ordinarily, it is preferable to treat a limited topic in depth than to provide a shallow or sketchy treatment of a broader subject. For instance, given a time limit of twenty minutes, you would likely not want to construct a speech around the purpose sentence, "My purpose is to tell my audience all they need to know to sell computers," to a group of newly hired sales reps. Such a grandiose topic demands far more time in order for the speaker to include product, industry, and competitive information, as well as instruction in sales techniques and how to effectively use them. In reality, twenty minutes might be enough time to cover a topic such as, "Five proven steps in *opening* a sales presentation."

RESEARCHING YOUR TOPIC

One of the most difficult and time-consuming tasks in speech preparation is finding solid sources of support with which to inform or persuade your audience. For this reason, less ambitious speakers may choose to speak only on that which they already know about their topic. This is a mistake. Whether you know a great deal or very little about your topic, a speech sprinkled with statistics, examples, quotations, or paraphrases from experts and illustrations from a variety of sources will enliven your talk, while at the same time showing your listeners you have done your homework and confirmed what you are saying. Audiences want to feel that a speaker has "earned the right to speak to them" and that he or she is not wasting their valuable time by telling them outdated or incorrect information. Even figures of national prominence typically include quotations, stories, analogies, and the like from respected sources.

Researching your topic involves determining what types of support you need to back up the claims or opinions you plan to present in your speech, searching in the library and using other valuable sources of support for the information you need, and recording the evidence you find in your search.

Understanding Different Types of Support

Whether the purpose of your speech is to provide information or to persuade your audience to adopt new views, what you are looking for in your research is support for the various statements you will be making. Support is needed mainly to prove the accuracy of your statements, but it can also be used to illustrate points and make them more interesting. Audiences are accustomed to listening for distinct kinds of support. Among the most common types are facts, statistics, testimony, narrative, examples, and comparisons.

FACTS. For backing up the accuracy of your statements, facts offer the strongest form of support. A fact is an event or a truth that is known to exist or has been observed. A fact is very difficult to contradict or refute, especially if it has been confirmed or witnessed by a large number of people. Here are examples of facts:

- The population of the U.S. is over 250 million.

- In 1993, our Gross Domestic Product was approximately $6.2 trillion.

- Between 1980 and 1990, the number of women in the U.S. salesforce increased by 42 percent.

Notice that a fact is always something that has occurred in the past or is presently occurring. No future event can be stated as a fact, because anything could happen to cancel or alter it.

STATISTICS. Statistics are a second useful form of support for accuracy of statements. Statistics are collections of facts stated in numerical terms. They can be used to present facts in percentages, rank order, and averages. The following are examples of statistics:

- In 1993, Americans spent $6.2 trillion. Twelve percent of that, or $744 billion, was spent on health care.

- Roughly 52 percent of the world's population is female and 48 percent is male.

- Eighty percent of Americans now consider themselves environmentalists at heart; 75 percent of Americans say they recycle cans; 60 percent say they recycle newspapers.

Most of us are familiar with the saying "It's easy to lie with statistics." Although the gathering of the statistics is indeed sometimes at fault, more often the speaker's interpretation of the numbers is what clouds complete truth. The only way to avoid such shady interpretations is to investigate every statistic objectively, then present it to your listeners according to your honest understanding.

TESTIMONY. Testimony, is the quoting or restating of another person's opinion to support a point. Often the person quoted is a recognized expert in the field. An example of a testimony is: "As Calvin Coolidge once said, 'The business of this country is business.'"

Since testimony is merely opinion, it is not as strong a form of support as facts are. Even when a quoted source is considered an expert, that expert can make a mistake. However, testimony is frequently useful, especially if you think your audience is likely to respect the views of the person you quote.

NARRATIVE. Narrative is supporting material in the form of a story, either real or imaginary. Besides being enjoyable and interesting, narratives are often used in a speech to help make a point that has already been or will soon be supported by facts or statistics. Here is an example of a brief story that might be told by a speaker who wished to talk about finding opportunities in one's own back yard:

> A story is told of Ali Hafed who sold his farm and set out in search of a diamond mine. He searched over the entire world without success and finally died in despair. One day, the man who had purchased his farm spotted a glittering object in his creek bed and soon became the owner of one of the world's richest diamond mines.

In addition to supporting the point you wish to make, stories maintain listener attention during the speech and aid audience recall afterwards.

EXAMPLES. Examples are specific instances or occurrences of a situation or principle you are attempting to describe. They are general kinds of support that can be stated in the form of facts, statistics, testimony, or narrative. Here is an example:

> A perfect example of a high-profile program that brings business and community together on a common environmental ground is the Scrapbox in Ann Arbor, Michigan. Businesses donate their

scrap material to a nonprofit organization that then offers the scrap material to the public for creative craft activities at home, in schools, in churches, or in senior citizen groups.

Examples may sometimes be used effectively to intensify or personalize your ideas. Notice how you are touched by this example of Ralph:

> There are many hungry families in our community who could benefit from food donations. Let me tell you about Ralph. Ralph is four years old. He has big brown eyes and a mop of black hair and an empty belly. In all his four years on this earth, Ralph has never once enjoyed three square meals in a single day.

COMPARISONS. Comparisons equate essentially unlike ideas or phrases. Put another way, they highlight the similarities that exist between basically dissimilar situations. Like examples, comparisons may take different forms. They may include facts, statistics, testimony, or narrative. They may also include the speaker's own opinions, if the opinions seem to offer a useful means of illustrating the views being presented. The following is an example of a comparison based on opinion:

> The way some people shop at their store reminds me of a swarm of bees clustered around a hive, each seemingly unaware of all the others crowded about.

Make Use of Support Materials Found in the Library

Most public or university libraries today, large or small, house an amazing array of information about nearly any subject on which you are likely to deliver a speech. Actually, with such a large amount of information now available to us on CD-ROM and Internet databases, in addition to the books in the stacks, the difficulty with library research may lie in finding the precise piece of data you need!

Unless you are familiar with libraries, you could wander around aimlessly, hoping to stumble over the piece of information you are seeking but with little or no idea how to find the trail that will lead to it. Once you know the key starting points, however, you can make the library work for you. Key starting points include the librarian, computerized research services, the card catalog, and the reference section.

LIBRARIAN. If you are not very familiar with library research, don't hesitate to approach one of the reference librarians. They are trained and paid to help people locate the starting point, which, most of the time, will eventually lead you to the information you need for your speech or presentation. If you lose the thread, return to the librarian and ask for help again.

COMPUTERIZED RESEARCH SERVICES. Most libraries now have some form of computerized search facilities for finding all types of information for speeches—even the highly specialized or obscure. What used to take hours to find by searching through volumes of periodical indexes, for example, can now be located in minutes by using CD-ROM (compact disk) databases. Many provide bibliographic information (that is, citations to books, articles, and other materials found elsewhere in the library). Others offer the full-text of articles, statistical data, and images. A list of helpful business-related CD-ROM databases is located in Exhibit 2.2. If you are not familiar with these services, ask a librarian for help in learning how to use them.

CARD CATALOG. Some libraries still use a card catalog as the master source for locating their information, although that number is shrinking rapidly. In the card catalog you will find three kinds of alphabetically ordered 3" x 5" cards for each book the library owns: a subject card, a title card, and an author card.

To use the card catalog if you know the book's title or the name of its author(s), you first look for a title card or an author card in the catalog. If the catalog contains a card with the book's title or author, you know that the library owns that book. You then write down the call number printed on the left-hand side of the card as your means of locating the book on the library shelves. When you are looking for books on a specific subject, such as "automobiles" or "surgery," not for a specific title or author, look in the alphabetized drawers of subject cards under the subject's category heading(s). The subject card will list one or more specific books on the subject with call numbers to help you locate them on the shelves.

Periodicals are also listed in the library's card catalog. If you are looking for a recent issue of a periodical, you can usually find it displayed on open shelves in the library's periodicals room. If you want an issue from a past year, the call number on the catalog card will direct you to the bookshelves where bound copies of older periodicals are kept.

REFERENCE SECTION. Suppose you are doing research for a speech dealing with Russian television viewing habits. You need very specific information, such as the number of TV sets purchased each year in Russia or the kinds of programs most commonly watched, but the library's card catalog contains few book or periodical titles that can help you. Or maybe you need to know about copyright law or what the average salary is for a dental hygienist. In any of these scenarios, you might spend hours searching through individual books and periodicals and still not find such specific information. Now is the time to discover the wealth of information that is available to you through the library's reference section. Although, as we have already discussed, much of this information is now available on CD-ROM,

EXHIBIT 2.2   Helpful Business-Related Databases

- *ABI/Inform*—bibliographic information on most business-related subjects, as well as companies, products, and industries.

- *Compendex* Plus*—engineering-related journal articles, technical reports, conference proceedings, and directories.

- *ERIC* (Educational Resources Information Center)—citations and abstracts to educational research, monographs, etc.

- *F & S Plus Text International*—information on international companies, products, markets and industries; selectively includes full-text and abstracts.

- *InfoTrac*—multidisciplinary index to 1,100 general and scholarly journals and major newspapers.

- *Statistical Masterfile*—index to statistical data published by the U.S. government, state governments, intergovernmental organizations, private organizations, trade associations, and university research bureaus.

much of it is not; therefore, it is important to know what information is housed in the reference section:

- **Encyclopedias.** You may have one of the general encyclopedias in your home, such as the *Encyclopedia Americana* or the *Encyclopedia Britannica*. Many libraries have these as well as several other general encyclopedias that cover all branches of knowledge. In addition, many libraries contain specialized encyclopedias dealing with certain fields, such as the *McGraw-Hill Encyclopedia of Science and Technology*, the *Encyclopedia of Psychology*, the *Encyclopedia of Education*, the *Encyclopedia of Religion and Ethics*, and *Grzimek's Animal Life Encyclopedia*, among others.

- **Yearbooks.** These are published annually and contain a tremendous amount of very detailed and concise information on a wide range of subjects. *The Facts on File Yearbook*, for instance, digests all the major national and international news events that occurred in a given year. *The World Almanac and Book of Facts* lists everything from the names of Nobel Prize winners since 1901 to sports records of college and pro teams. If you are interested in statistical information about the social, economic, and political aspects of life in the United States, you can discover such facts as the United States birth and death rates and median family income, broken down by state.

- **Biographical Aids.** The reference section also contains collections of biographical sketches of noted persons, both living and dead. *Who's Who in America, Who's Who of American Women, International Who's Who,* and the *Dictionary of American Biography* are several of the leading sources of biographical information about famous individuals. *Biography Index,* published four times each year, indexes biographical material that has appeared in certain books and periodicals. It is especially helpful if you need information about important living people.

- **Atlases.** Whenever geography is an important aspect of your speech topic, you will want to check an atlas. In addition to the usual maps of the world and each state in the United States, atlases provide you with information about the climate, energy, and food resources of the various parts of our world and even treat the universe beyond. Two of the best known atlases are *Times Atlas of the World, Comprehensive Edition,* and the *Rand McNally Cosmopolitan World Atlas.*

- **Periodicals Indexes.** Once you have a general notion of the direction in which you wish to go with your topic, you will find more detailed discussions of it in periodicals, newspapers, and books. Several handy reference works list articles in periodicals under general subject headings. *The Reader's Guide to Periodical Literature* lists articles in current magazines, such as *Newsweek, Reader's Digest, Time,* and *U.S. News & World Report.* If your topic deals with business, references such as *Accounting and Tax Index, Business Periodicals Index,* and *Index to Legal Periodicals* may be helpful.

  In addition to searching for information specific to your current needs, feel free to generally browse in the periodicals section of your library. Looking at pictures in magazines can stimulate your interest in topics you might someday be asked to speak about. Regular reading, especially of magazines dealing with current events and issues, can provide you with a constant awareness of important subjects.

  Newspapers, of course, provide additional sources of information. Even though you may not subscribe to *The New York Times,* you may discover supportive information for your speech by checking in the *New York Times Index.* By so doing, you can learn the date on which the story of interest appeared in *The New York Times,* then check that same date for that report in most metropolitan dailys.

- **Quotations.** Speakers can also find quotations to support their ideas in sources such as *Bartlett's Familiar Quotations, Brewer's Dictionary of Phrase and Fable, Granger's Index to Poetry,* and the *Oxford Dictionary of Quotations.*

GOVERNMENT DOCUMENTS SECTION. There are publications related to nearly every subject field in the government documents section. As the name implies, government information—international, federal, state, and local laws; congressional hearings; and technical reports, rules, and regulations—comprises a large part of the collection. In addition, you will find a wide variety of other types of government publications, including census and statistical data for nearly every imaginable topic, national trade data, environmental impact statements, and reports from international organizations.

Finding Other Sources of Support

Although the library will often provide you with much of the information you need for a speech or presentation, do not overlook other valuable sources of information, including Internet resources, interviews, television and radio programs, newspapers, informal surveys, and information published or provided by special-interest groups.

INTERNET RESOURCES. The Internet is essentially a network of networks that can interconnect your personal computer with more than 3.5 million other computers worldwide. No one person or organization is in charge of the Internet. It runs through the collective efforts of many thousands of individuals and organizations around the world. Internet users have access to library catalogs and databases, software programs, images, electronic books and journals, satellite weather maps, electronic mail and discussion groups, and more.

You can gain access to the Internet by subscribing to a commercial service such as America OnLine, Compuserve, or Prodigy, each of which has its own resident set of databases, journals, and discussion groups. You can also access the Internet via the World Wide Web, a navigation program for accessing information from any source throughout the Internet. The easiest way to begin using the Web is to purchase a software package called a "web browser," such as *Netscape Navigator, Mosaic,* or *Netcruiser,* to name a few.

INTERVIEWS. Interviews with people who are knowledgeable about your topic can prove to be very helpful. If your topic concerns entrepreneurship, why not interview a local business owner? If your topic has to do with health-care costs, you might contact your local or state medical association. Such sources, generated by telephone calls and face-to-face encounters, usually have a greater impact on an audience than do library sources alone.

TELEVISION AND RADIO PROGRAMS. Other frequently overlooked sources of support for speeches are television and radio—particularly news programs. Since the main purpose of local and network news teams is to gather and sort out facts and testimony, their reports are often replete with information with which to support your ideas. Regularly keeping up with world and local news and jotting down both the date of the program and the specific source can prove quite useful when you are called upon to speak on a topic with which you are not thoroughly familiar.

NEWSPAPERS. Because newspapers are available for reading at any time, they possess an advantage over television and radio as sources of supporting materials. If you happen to miss a particular news broadcast, you often fail to obtain the information later. A newspaper, on the other hand, can be retrieved and read months or even years later.

INFORMAL SURVEYS. Taking your own informal survey of public opinion among friends or neighbors can also prove an effective type of support for a speech, particularly when you speak on local issues. Audiences are impressed when a speaker is sufficiently enthusiastic about the issues to conduct such a survey; they enjoy hearing what people living in their own city or town think about a topic.

SPECIAL-INTEREST GROUPS. When you are speaking on a controversial topic, you can frequently write to special-interest groups to obtain information to support one side of an issue. On highly controversial topics, you should also write to interest groups that are opposed to you position in order to respond effectively to their claims. Of course, you need to realize that information sent to you by special-interest groups is bound to be biased in favor of their particular position on the issue involved. You can also obtain a great deal of information from government agencies on myriad topics ranging from science to law to education. If you do not know where to write to obtain materials, contact your congressional representative's office. Writing away for such information naturally means that you have to start your speech preparation well in advance to allow time for the information to reach you.

Recording Your Evidence

As you discover facts, statistics, testimony, and other forms of support for your speech, be sure to write them down. Even though you may not be certain you will use a particular piece of evidence in your speech, record it and the source where you discovered it anyway. Always transcribe more than you plan to use to avoid making extra trips to the library or rescheduling an interview.

It is best to establish a consistent system for recording speech evidence. Most speakers prefer to take their notes on 3" x 5" index cards, recording only one item of information on each card. These can be arranged later in the best order for presentation and are easy to handle on the platform. When you discover an item of information you think might be useful, first record a general heading for it at the top left-hand corner of the card, then the specific source from which you obtained it. In the center of the card, place the quotation, example, statistic, or fact. Sometimes the evidence may spill over to the back of the card or even to a second card. During the actual presentation of the speech, it is usually better to announce the source before the evidence.

Typing the cards you decide to use during delivery is useful, since it makes them easy to read on the platform. However, if your handwriting is clear and legible, typing is not necessary. Also, as an alternative to taking notes on 3" x 5" cards, you can enter your notes in a computer word processing, presentation, or organization application. Your notes can then be shuffled or reorganized as you see fit and printed in a 3" x 5" format for your actual speech.

Even when you are not preparing for a specific speech, you may find it helpful to keep a general file of favorite topics for future use. You can build a storehouse of information to support those topics by gathering quotations, statistics, and other forms of evidence from books, magazines, newspapers, television, or conversation. A person interested in current events can usually spot information that may prove useful the next time a speech is needed.

ORGANIZING AND OUTLINING YOUR SPEECH

As you go about researching your speech topic, you will simultaneously be deciding on an organizational pattern for your presentation. Once your overall pattern has been selected, you are then ready to write an outline of your topic.

Selecting a Pattern of Speech Organization

Although you are obviously free to arrange your speech materials in any manner you choose, over the years certain methods of arrangement have proved effective for particular occasions and audiences. Your specific speech purpose will also have a great deal to do with the type of organizational pattern you select.

CHRONOLOGICAL SPEECHES. One common organizational pattern for speeches is the chronological pattern. This arrangement proceeds from past to present to future; in other words, the speech develops in the same order in which the events developed in time. Notice in the following example how the speaker makes his point about the use of technology in the future by talking first about how it has hurt us in the past:

> In ancient times the use of fire and the domestication of plants and animals greatly enhanced man's ability to feed and clothe himself. Later, irrigation and other forms of water management were key to the establishment of advanced civilizations in Mesopotamia and along the Nile. The use of these technologies also engendered massive and sometimes detrimental changes in the environment. In Mesopotamia, unwise irrigation practices eventually ruined the topsoil; in the Middle East and elsewhere, the overgrazing of arid land turned untold millions of previously productive acres into useless desert. . . . There is no doubt that technology is vital to our existence. The question is where we should go from here. Looking at what man has done in the past with his hands, mind, and tools, I am convinced that technology can in the future be utilized to alleviate or eliminate our major social and economic problems, and that we have both the will and the ability to deal with any undesirable side effects.

A speech in chronological order need not always contain all three time periods: past, present, and future. The essential feature of this pattern is that the ideas or events in the speech move forward according to a time sequence.

SPATIAL SPEECHES. When the parts of a speech are tied together by space arrangements rather than by time sequence, the organizational pattern is called spatial. It is useful in speeches in which the speaker describes a place. For instance, if you were asked to give a presentation familiarizing workers with the layout of a new plant they were about to occupy but had not yet seen, you would use spatial organization, describing each section of the new plant in order. Very likely you would also use a floor plan or pictures of the new plant as visual aids to improve your listeners' understanding.

TOPICAL SPEECHES. A third organizational pattern, called topical, is also frequently used. This is a broadly defined pattern in which the speech topic is broken down into its natural parts. An example would be a presentation describing your company's divisions and the various departments within each division. A speech about salesforce organization is another example of a topical speech because it would very likely be divided into discussions about telemarketing, field sales, national accounts, and the like. In short, as long as the divisions represent natural parts of the whole topic, the organizational pattern is called topical.

PROBLEM-SOLUTION SPEECHES. The problem-solution pattern is still another pattern used in speech making. Here the speaker devotes roughly the first half of the speech to describing a problem that exists or is about to occur and the second half developing one or more solutions. If, for instance, the problem is that an organization's personnel costs are rising at a faster rate than its productivity, then the president might spend the first half of the speech time proving how serious the problem is and the second half outlining an exit interview policy that would better utilize the company's human resources. Sometimes speakers misuse this organizational pattern by spending nearly the entire time discussing the problem and then barely mentioning the solution in the final statements of the speech. It is best to devote approximately equal time to the problem and the solution(s).

MONROE'S MOTIVATED SEQUENCE SPEECHES. Another pattern used especially by salespersons is called Monroe's Motivated Sequence. This pattern was originally suggested by Alan H. Monroe for use in persuasive speeches. It consists of five separate steps, which are illustrated in Exhibit 2.3:

1. The Attention Step
2. The Need Step
3. The Satisfaction Step
4. The Visualization Step
5. The Action Step

The first step is an obvious one. Gaining the audience's attention is always the first task for any speaker in any type of speech situation. Once the listeners are paying close attention, the second step is for the speaker to show the audience that they have needs not being met by the way things are at present. The third step in Monroe's Motivated Sequence is to present the opinion or solution that will satisfy these unmet needs. In the fourth step, the speaker helps the listeners visualize the change that will occur if they adopt his or her views. Finally, in the fifth step, the speaker tells the listeners what action they must take to bring about the improvement he or she has promised. Speakers trying to persuade an audience often use the five steps of Monroe's Motivated Sequence to organize their presentations.

STRING-OF-BEADS SPEECHES. The string-of-beads organizational pattern is used primarily for after-dinner speeches or speeches to entertain. This pattern consists of a series of stories, jokes, or anecdotes strung out like beads on a string and tied loosely to some weak central theme. The jokes or anecdotes themselves usually carry the main impact in this kind of speech,

EXHIBIT 2.3   Monroe's Motivated Sequence

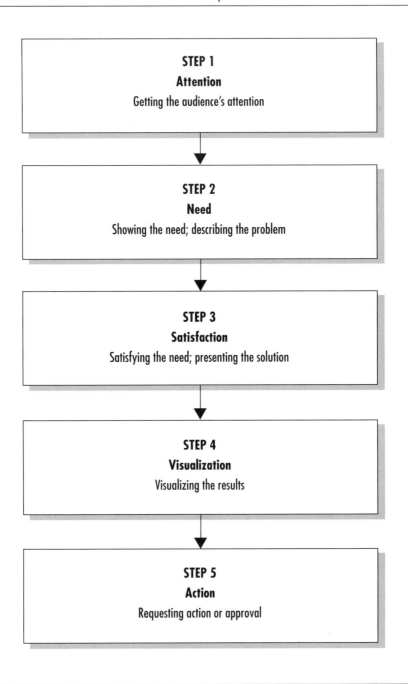

and the topic or theme is less important. An advantage of this pattern for an after-dinner speaker is its flexibility. Should a speech run overtime, the speaker can easily dispense with several anecdotes without the audience feeling that the speech is unfinished. This pattern does not ordinarily work well, however, for other types of speaking.

Constructing an Outline

A good outline can be likened to a tree without its leaves. All the basics are present in the tree—the base (the purpose sentence), the necessary support (the main heads), and the division into branches (the subheads). The leaves represent the full sentences you add when you actually make the presentation.

PURPOSE SENTENCE. If your speech outline is to have any order to it, you must know clearly what your purpose is in making the speech. The best way to begin a clear speech outline is by writing at the top of your outline the purpose sentence you selected earlier. Remember that the purpose sentence states exactly what you hope to accomplish by giving the speech: what you hope your listeners will know, think, believe, or do as a result of hearing your speech. Imagine that your general purpose is to tell your listeners something about the critical skills needed by new hires in today's business environment. With this general speech purpose in mind, you might generate a number of very different specific speech purposes:

- The purpose of this speech is to inform my listeners about the critical need for employees with good writing skills.
- The purpose of the speech is to convince my college audience that they are unlikely to be hired without basic computer literacy.
- The purpose of my speech is to urge my listeners to pick up fluency in a language other than English if they wish to be promoted in international business.

Notice that each of these purpose sentences states a specific idea about which a person might wish to speak. A purpose sentence such as "To inform my audience about 'new hires'" is useless—it is not a complete thought and thus carries no punch as a purpose. It also demonstrates that the speaker does not have a *specific* purpose in mind, only a general topic. By the time you begin outlining, you must have a specific purpose in mind. The purpose sentence serves to guide you as you complete your outline.

Sometimes speakers think of a purpose sentence as a key sentence that is phrased for use at the beginning of the speech. Although you may often state aloud the same general idea at the start of the spoken speech, the purpose sentence itself is really a *written* sentence meant only to guide your outlining process. When a speaker states the purpose aloud to the listeners, it is usually reworded in a much more conversational style.

MAIN HEADS. The major divisions of a speech outline are referred to as main heads. Main heads are designated with Roman numerals—I, II, III, and so on. Ordinarily the fewer main divisions you make of your topic, the better. In fact, most speeches should have only two or three main heads, although there are exceptions to this rule. A topic with eight or nine divisions, however, becomes too difficult for the audience to follow or remember and hard for the speaker to fit into the time limit. If it seems impossible to avoid dividing your topic into a large number of main heads, you should consider narrowing the scope of your topic or combining several heads into one.

Suppose you are a CEO outlining a policy speech dealing with a fresh approach to performance review across all levels of your organization. Your purpose sentence might read:

> My purpose is to show my listeners the benefits of moving to a Management by Objectives (MBO) approach to performance appraisal.

Three main headings of your talk might look something like this:

I. MBO focuses on past performance as a springboard to setting future objectives.

II. An MBO approach is typically more concrete and measurable than most other approaches.

III. MBO provides an additional level of motivation for employees to constantly improve.

As illustrated in the example above, each main head should directly support the purpose sentence and be approximately equal in importance.

SUBHEADS. Subheads relate to main heads in the same manner that main heads relate to the purpose sentence. They subdivide each main head into parallel and approximately equal parts. Subheads are designated by capital letters—A, B, C, and so on. Notice how the following subheads support the first main head in the speech on MBO:

I. MBO focuses on past performance as a springboard to setting future objectives.

   A. Objectives not completely met in a past performance period may limit the number of new objectives for an upcoming period.

B. Long-range objectives (beyond a single performance period) can be planned as carry-over in order to accomplish larger achievements.

C. Past performance also serves as a means by which supervisors can plan employees' career paths through the organization.

While it is possible to further subdivide the ideas of the outline under subheads, this is not ordinarily done. Most of the subdivisions below the subheads are reserved for supporting details (examples, statistics, narratives, comparisons, etc.) rather than for concepts or ideas. Usually these are included only as single words or brief phrases, not as complete sentences. They are designated by Arabic numerals—i, ii, iii, and so on.

COMPLETE SENTENCES FOR MAIN HEADS AND SUBHEADS. Main heads and first-level subheads in speech outlines should be stated as complete sentences. Although experienced speakers sometimes use word or phrase outlines, full-sentence outlines are best for beginning speakers. Writing out the basic ideas in complete thoughts forces you to think through the ideas and also helps set them in your memory. This does not mean, however, that the sentences should be lengthy. Actually, you should strive to keep them as brief and simple as possible, as long as they are grammatically complete. Single words or brief phrases will suffice for your supporting data.

Once it is completed, your outline gives you a clear picture of the ideas of your speech in two ways: First, you see the relative importance of ideas by the way in which main and subideas are indented on the page; second, the use of Roman numerals for main heads, capital letters for subheads, and Arabic numerals for supporting information helps further imbed the pattern of ideas in your mind. And, of course, since you prepared your own outline, you generally become familiar with it by the time you have completed writing it.

REHEARSING YOUR SPEECH

Rehearsal is the crowning point of speech preparation. Nothing can take the place of thorough practice, and if well done, rehearsal can put you in top form for a successful speech. Without it, a speaker is like a golfer who has not played regularly for the past four months entering the U.S. Open.

One or two brief run-throughs does not constitute thorough rehearsal. Start preparing your speech well before the speaking date and allow time for several rehearsal sessions. Rehearsal that is crammed into one evening is far less effective than three or four rehearsal sessions on successive nights.

In order to prepare yourself maximally for a speech you must progress through several rehearsal stages, developing gradually from the stage in which ideas are simply listed on your outline to the point where they are firmly implanted in your mind. Since people's brains work subconsciously on such ideas between rehearsal sessions, you need to find the time and place for well-spaced rehearsals if you are to have total command of the speech material.

Finding the Right Place for Rehearsal

Since your actual speech or presentation will be spoken aloud, you need to rehearse in a place where you can speak aloud. Saying the speech to yourself or whispering it quietly only allows you to practice the mental parts of the speech—the ideas. But, as we will discuss in detail in Chapter 4, public speaking demands a number of physical skills as well. You need to rehearse proper breathing and voice projection, clear articulation, good timing, and correct synchronization of words with body movements. The ancient Greek orator Demosthenes is reported to have rehearsed his speeches on the seashore where he had to speak over the roar of the surf. It is also said that he practiced with pebbles in his mouth to make himself conscious of the need for clear articulation. Don't risk choking by using pebbles but do consider practicing outdoors because you will be forced to speak above the noise of wind and traffic. If you cannot find a suitable place outdoors, the next best place is a room similar in size and acoustics to the one in which you will give the actual speech.

Planting the Pattern of Ideas in Your Mind

Begin by reading your outline over silently to yourself several times, trying to set the pattern of ideas in your mind. Often the major segments of the outline will already be fixed in your mind because of the familiarity you naturally gained with the material as you wrote it.

Once you have the ideas firmly planted in your mind, stand up and say the ideas aloud to an imaginary audience. Speak the ideas in whatever words come to you as you are rehearsing, but be sure they are clear and concrete (we'll talk more about word choice in Chapter 3). Try to go through the entire speech, filling in details of the outline without starting over. Your speech will be halting and full of long pauses at first, but it will begin to smooth out with repeated practice. Each time you go through the speech, try to say the ideas in different ways. Remember, what you are doing is planting a pattern of ideas in your mind, not a memorized pattern of words. We'll talk in detail about memorization versus other methods of delivery in Chapter 4.

Have your outline or note cards handy (whichever you plan to use during the actual speech) and refer to them if you forget an idea. Run through the entire speech five to ten times or until you are certain you can go from beginning to end without hesitation. This will help establish your pattern of ideas securely in your mind.

Rehearsing Alone and with Friends

Most people prefer to rehearse a speech alone, at least until they have it pretty well smoothed out. Once you feel you have the speech under control, however, rehearsing with a friend or a couple of colleagues or family members as your audience can improve your preparation. Having a dress rehearsal of this type can give you ideas about possible audience reactions you cannot obtain through a solo rehearsal: Are you speaking loudly enough to be heard in all parts of the room? Do the listeners react in an unexpected way to a particular portion of your speech? Do they follow the organization of your speech? Do they understand all of the message? Do they agree or disagree with all or part of your message? Knowing the answers to these kinds of questions beforehand can allow you time to make changes and produce a better effect on your real audience.

Timing Rehearsals

Time yourself as you practice. Using a watch or other timing device that shows how much time has been spent and how much is left can be helpful. The timing will probably not be too precise in the first few run-throughs, but by your final practice session you should be able to conclude your speech within thirty seconds of your time limit. Bear in mind that if you are giving a thirty-minute speech, two or three minutes' leeway will probably be permissible; however, if you are scheduled to speak on a radio or television program, you will need to keep close track of your timing and may even prefer to use a script for rehearsal rather than an outline.

Using Note Cards

When the time for delivering your speech arrives, it is usually best to transfer the contents of your preparation outline onto 3" x 5" or 4" x 6" note cards in a briefer form. These note cards should contain all the major headings and subheadings from the full sentence outline but expressed in the form of single words or brief phrases. In addition to the major ideas, the note cards should contain all of the statistics, examples, quotations, and other forms of evidence you plan to cite during your speech.

CHAPTER THREE

Choosing Effective Language: The Speaker's Ultimate Tool

Speeches are made of ideas, but unless those ideas are expressed in carefully selected language, they may be overlooked. The words you choose to speak are the garments with which you clothe your ideas; therefore, choosing effective language for a speech is like choosing the right clothes for a special occasion. Words can be courageous or timid, commanding or pleading, persuasive or entertaining, hurtful or kind. Their effect on the listeners can be enormous or microscopic depending on how well the words clothe the ideas. In this chapter, you will find a number of suggestions that can help you choose the kind of language that will best express your ideas to a given audience.

You may ask, "Does this mean I should write out my speeches word for word, then read or memorize them?" No, not usually. Most speech experts today believe you should learn to give the majority of your speeches extemporaneously—outlining the ideas beforehand but choosing the precise wording during the speech itself. Linda and Dick Heun, authors of a college speech text, put it this way:

> The main reason for not writing out a speech and reading (or memorizing) it is that your focus then would be on your wording rather than your audience's reactions. One unique advantage of oral communication is that you have direct eye contact with your audience and can watch, interpret, and adapt to its reactions.
>
> A second reason for not writing out your speech is that oral style is quite different from written style. In fact, Charles Fox, noted British politician and orator of the nineteenth century, once said, "Does it read well? Then it's not a good speech."

On some occasions, of course, you may need to speak from a manuscript. But for the most part, this chapter's immediate benefit to you will be in showing you how to select effective language for those sections of your speech in which you want to make the greatest impression—the introduction, the conclusion, and some occasional high points you may wish to read or memorize. In working on the language of these special parts of your speeches, you will also be gaining the skill to put words together effectively when speaking extemporaneously. Specifically, in this chapter you will explore the five qualities of spoken language that make it different from written language. Being aware of these differences will help you state your message clearly. We will then discuss several ways to emphasize important points in your speech and how to effectively use figures of speech. Finally, we will consider some common language-related problems of public speaking and how to avoid them.

MAKING SPOKEN LANGUAGE CLEAR

The first step in choosing effective language for public speaking is to realize that language that is appropriate for writing is not always appropriate for speaking. In part this is because the tasks of reading and listening are so different. Readers can set their own pace, stopping and reviewing anything that is hard to understand. Listeners, on the other hand, must try to keep up with the speaker. If they miss an idea, it is often gone for good.

Effective language for speaking must therefore be simple, brief, and clear enough that listeners can easily understand it.

In general, spoken language possesses five specific qualities that make it very different from written language:

1. Spoken language makes greater use of short and simple words.
2. Spoken language tends to be more concrete, less abstract.
3. Spoken language is usually more specific.
4. Spoken language makes greater use of restatement.
5. Spoken language generally includes fewer unnecessary words.

This section focuses on these five qualities of spoken language. Although they are a natural part of conversational spoken language, they are too often forgotten when it comes to giving public speeches.

Keeping Wording Short and Simple

Spoken sentences need to be shorter and simpler than written ones. A great number of long sentences make a speech difficult for listeners to follow. They also make it harder for your audience to maintain attention for any length of time.

Say each of these sentences aloud, then decide which would be easier for a listening audience to grasp quickly:

- We have gathered here today in order to explain and detail for you the reasons why one of our very own co-workers deserves to be selected as the next chairperson of our quality work team.

- We're here to tell you why our co-worker, Sheila Cox, should be the next chairperson of our quality work team.

Both sentences impart essentially the same message, right? But wouldn't you be more likely to understand the second sentence if someone spoke it to you?

The use of simple words has long been considered a sign of clear language. Simple words are not always short words, although many are indeed short; rather, simple words are those that are among the ordinary vocabulary of your particular audience on any given occasion. When speaking to your peers—people in roughly your own age group and with a similar level of education—your selection of language is relatively easy. Simply choose words you would typically use in conversation yourself. When speaking to a much younger audience or to a less-educated group of listeners, on the other hand, adjust your language level downward appropriately. Were you asked, for example, to speak to a fourth-grade class about computers, which of these sentences would you choose?

- The type of communication protocol existing between your systems unit and printer may present you with a critical consideration for the proper operation of your computer.

- You need to know a little bit about how your computer talks with your printer if you want to use your computer well.

If you address a special group with a vocabulary of its own—a sports group or a medical group, perhaps—it is permissible to use the special words of that group as long as the entire audience will understand the language used. The same is true when addressing groups composed of audience members from a specific region or cultural group. The basic rule of thumb is this: As long as you are a member of the group to which you are speaking and nearly all your listeners understand the special regional or cultural terms, you should feel free to use them. Actually, you compliment such an audience by using language that is special to you and to them. Do not, however, try to use the regional or cultural language of a special group if you are not a member of the group or if there are many nonmembers in your audience.

Using Concrete Language

Language for public speaking must not only be simple, it must also be concrete. Concrete words and phrases are the kind that let the listener "see" the ideas as well as understand them. A word such as *girl* is concrete because it stands for something that can be perceived by the senses. Conversely, a word such as *beautiful* is abstract because you cannot see, touch, feel, smell, or taste *beautiful*. Compare the following two sentences and decide which one gives you a clearer mental picture of the ideas expressed:

- John seemed nervous, yet determined.

- John was shaking, but his jaw was tightly set.

Although the two sentences express essentially the same ideas, the second sentence allows you to "see" those ideas. You can't see *nervous* but you can develop a mental image of a person *shaking* nervously. Now compare the next two sentences and decide for yourself which is more concrete and which is more abstract:

- The taste in Katie's mouth was like frozen strawberries slowly melting on her tongue.

- The taste in Katie's mouth was cold and tantalizing.

Using Specific Words

A public speaker also needs to use specific words. Specific words are words that refer to a limited class of objects. For example, the word *president* is a more specific word than *manager* since there are many kinds of managers in business who are not presidents. In other words, while all presidents are managers, not all managers are presidents; therefore, the class *president* is smaller and more specific than the class *manager.* Note, however, that a given word cannot be labeled general or specific in a vacuum—it will merely be more general or more specific than some other word. We just said that *president* is more specific than *manager.* But *manager* is more specific than *administrator,* which includes the class manager. Notice the progression from general to specific in Exhibit 3.1. When you are preparing a speech, the trick is to pick the most specific word you can find to tell your audience just what you have in mind.

Restating Main Ideas

Restatement is a natural speaking device that assures you that the listener does not miss or forget a part of your message. Writers have less need to restate because the reader can carry out any necessary review by simply rereading a phrase or sentence. Since listeners do not have this opportunity, public speakers typically restate their main ideas a good deal, using

EXHIBIT 3.1   Use the Right Word for the Right Group

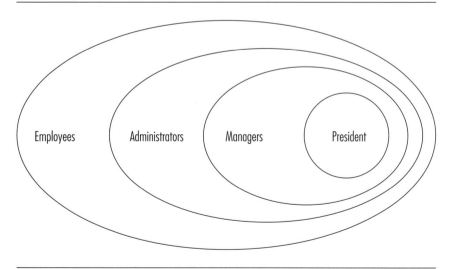

somewhat different language each time to assure that everyone gets the idea.

Removing Unnecessary Words

In daily life, being economical means not wasting money or other resources. In public speaking, being economical means not wasting words. Part of clear speaking consists of using as few words as necessary to get the message across. Once you have accomplished that, stop!

Did you know that on the same occasion that Abraham Lincoln delivered the Gettysburg Address, another speaker, Edward Everett, also gave a speech. Lincoln's speech, only ten sentences in length, took about two minutes to deliver. Everett's lasted two hours. Perhaps you have not heard of Edward Everett or his speech, but Lincoln's Gettysburg Address is known around the world. Part of the reason for the lasting effect of Lincoln's speech was undoubtedly his economy of language. Afterwards, Everett wrote Lincoln a letter in which he declared that he wished that he could have done as much justice to the occasion with his two-hour speech as Lincoln had with his two-minute one.

One of the best means of achieving economy of language is by chopping needless words from individual sentences. The speaker who says, "We must take into consideration the fact that this property comes under certain zoning restrictions," could save words (and energy) by shortening the wording, "We must consider certain zoning restrictions on this property." Consider two other examples:

> **Uneconomical:** Regarding the situation in the flooded area, we must make a concerted effort to aid the local residents.
>
> **Economical:** We must try to aid the residents in the flooded area.
>
> **Uneconomical:** A period of sunny weather set in and remained for a whole week.
>
> **Economical:** We had sunshine for a whole week.

In each of these examples, many of the words in the uneconomical versions are not needed. They do not add anything to the meaning of the sentence. They are unnecessary and should be left out.

CREATING LEVELS OF EMPHASIS

So far we have considered the importance of using clear language when speaking in public. Language must also help make a speech memorable. Listeners will be more likely to remember your message if you choose language that emphasizes its important points.

Several language devices can be used to create levels of emphasis. Their purpose is to highlight certain parts of your speech and thereby downplay the other parts of the speech where they are not used. Among the most common devices used to create emphasis are contrast, rhetorical questions, repetition, and climax. Before you consider these devices, however, consider the most basic way of creating different levels of emphasis—the use of variety.

Using Variety

Without variety in words and types of sentences, a speech quickly forms a repetitious language pattern. Any kind of regularly recurring pattern distracts an audience, causing its members to pay less attention to the speaker's message. But when there is variety in word usage and sentence length, certain points will stand out and others will recede into the background. Thus, language variety can be of great use in creating levels of emphasis.

Varying one's vocabulary, sentence length, and sentence structure can also help maintain listener interest. It can enliven your speech. Speakers who repeatedly use the same words to refer to a given idea soon sound monotonous. Likewise, speakers who use only short, simple sentences begin to sound like machine guns chattering. And those who use only long sentences quickly lose the attention and interest of their listeners. A basic key to successful speaking is variety.

Employing Contrast

The language device called *contrast* has long been used to make important statements stick in listeners' minds. Contrast is not an easy device to create. It begins with two balanced phrases, clauses, or sentences. The words containing the ideas the speaker wishes to emphasize are the only words changed or rearranged in the second part of the statement. But ordinarily speakers do not spout forth well-balanced statements of contrast on the spur of the moment. Such statements usually grow from extended thought and careful planning. Therefore, contrast is usually found when a speaker has had ample time to plan precise language. If you plan to use contrast, you will need to think the thought through before the speech and then use a manuscript or note cards showing the statements of contrast you wish to make. The time spent is not likely to be wasted. Well-planned use of contrast can prove effective in most speeches. Consider the following use of contrast in a speech on industrial pollution:

> If industry proves unwilling to save the environment, over the long haul the environment will prove unable to sustain industry.

Contrast, however, is a device that can be easily overused. Since it is generally saved to emphasize one of the major points in a speech, overusing it can quickly cause you to stress too many points in your speech. As a result, the audience may become confused and forget *all* of them. One or two well-placed statements of contrast are ample, even in a lengthy speech.

Including Rhetorical Questions

Ideas in a speech can also be emphasized by putting them in the form of rhetorical questions. Rhetorical questions are questions that are not generally meant to be answered out loud. But because it is difficult for most people to ignore a question put to them, they will generally try to answer it in their minds and thus begin thinking about your topic. In the following example, the speaker used a series of rhetorical questions at the onset of his speech to set the tone for the message he planned to deliver:

> There are three basic questions relative to the strategic quality planning category: First, how do you approach quality improvement? Second, how do you plan your business using quality strategies? Third, how do you know you're successful?

The speaker did not expect his audience to respond aloud to these questions; however, by asking the questions at the beginning of his speech, he did provoke his audience to think about the answers and thus created a mindset for his speech.

Making Use of Repetition

Repetition—stating the same idea using the same words—is another effective device for highlighting important points. Listening to TV commercials, you might wonder whether modern television advertising ever makes use of any device other than repetition. Public speakers also make regular use of repetition. Sometimes their basic purpose in using it is to persuade, to create an emotional reaction, or to aid listener recall. In many cases, however, the basic purpose is to emphasize important points. When used in this way, its effect is like holding up a large sign stating: "Don't miss this! It's one of the most important points of my speech."

Repetition is not the same as restatement. As we discussed earlier in the chapter, restatement aids listener recall by using *different* words to state the *same* idea, but it ordinarily does not drive a point home to the same extent that repetition does. Because you use the *same* words repeatedly, repetition is much more effective in signaling the important point for the audience. It sounds an emphatic note of insistence that is nearly impossible to ignore. Use repetition sparingly, however. Its overuse is very annoying, and it serves as a highly effective means of achieving emphasis only so long as it is not overused.

A variation of repetition consists of beginning or ending sentences with the same single word or short phrase. This device, called *parallelism,* was used by Lee Iacocca in a speech to the National Press Club in which he announced that Chrysler was paying off its federally guaranteed loans seven years early (the italics are his):

> I *learned,* and I hope all of you did. I *learned* that a little sacrifice shared equally goes a long way.

> I *learned* that we *can* compete, even in the darkest days, with anybody.

> I *learned* that when adversarial positions melt under pressure, good things happen.

> I even *learned* that an ad hoc industrial policy is better than no policy at all.

Like repetition, parallelism must be used sparingly in order to be effective.

Ordering Items in Series for Maximum Effect

When a speaker lists three or four items in a series, the last item referred to carries the greatest emphasis. Suppose you wished to emphasize how seriously wrong someone's behavior has been. You might order your statement like this, "His behavior is wrong, it is immoral, it is actually criminal." This is called *climax ordering*—moving from less significant to more significant and ending the series with whichever item is most important. If, in the example above, you were to arrange the items in any other order, the audience would most likely become confused.

Since audiences usually expect to hear climax ordering whenever items spoken in a series differ in importance, speakers can emphasize the most important item simply by placing it last. The late AFL-CIO leader George Meany used climax ordering at the conclusion of his classic 1956 Labor Day radio address to emphasize the goals of the trade union movement. Notice that the goals (shown here in italics) increase in importance as Meany draws nearer to the conclusion of his speech:

> On this Labor Day, the trade union movement dedicates itself to work for peace, with freedom and justice for mankind—to work for *a steadily higher standard of living*—to work for the *full enjoyment of civil rights by all Americans,* regardless of race, color

or religion—to work for *improved relations between labor and management* under a law that will be fair to both—to work for *a broader measure of social security* for the protection of all citizens against the hazards of poverty, old age, disability, and illness—to work, in short, for *the highest ideals of the land we love.*

As is the case with most language devices used for creating levels of emphasis, climax ordering must be used sparingly. Well-placed usage of such devices, however, can make the difference between a poor speech and an excellent one.

USING FIGURES OF SPEECH

Language in a speech must sometimes be rich and imaginative and at other times, plain and straightforward. The plainer parts help emphasize the richer ones. Few speakers can produce clever, imaginative language constantly, and even if they could, the listeners would soon sicken of it. It would be much like eating steak every day, without the faintest hope of some ordinary hamburger now and then. The moderated and careful use of imaginative language can, however, add a great deal to your speeches. Knowing ways of creating rich language can help you make your ideas clearer to your listeners.

In this section, we'll look at several methods of making speech more imaginative through the use of figures of speech. Figures of speech are phrases and sentences that make a point by stating something that is not literally or exactly true. They rely for their impact on comparison, contrast, and exaggeration to make meanings clear.

Using Similes and Metaphors

Two special forms of comparison, the simile and the metaphor, are frequently used to make ideas memorable for the listeners. A simile is a brief comparison of two basically unlike things, using the word *like* or *as*. In the following simile, the speaker conjures up an image of how difficult it is to maintain quality by comparing the effort to running a marathon:

> Quality is like a marathon; it involves a lot of hard work day after day and you can't let up.

A metaphor is a more direct comparison of two things than a simile, because it omits the word *like* or *as*. In the following example, the speaker uses a rather vivid metaphor to liken public debt to something equally unpleasant:

I get despondent about that deficit because I see us burying our kids in a dung heap of public debt.

Similes and metaphors are usually only one sentence in length. For instance, the often-heard retort of a jokester whose joke has fallen flat is a one-sentence simile: "Well, that went over like a lead balloon!" At other times, a simile or metaphor may consist of several sentences. Hubert Farbes won a national speech contest with a speech containing this combination of metaphor-simile:

For there is a parasite in the minds of men today. It grows like a leech, taking its morbid existence from the strength of its host, warping his mind and character.

If a comparison grows beyond two or three sentences, however, it is ordinarily labeled an extended comparison or an analogy. Similes and metaphors gain part of their impact from being short and pithy.

Similes and metaphors may be used fairly frequently in a speech. This does no harm, as long as the speaker does not stuff the listener with such devices. Keep in mind that a substantial portion of your speech must consist of plain food, so that the special treat may be appreciated.

Experimenting with Personification

Personification is a figure of speech in which a speaker gives human qualities to inanimate objects, ideas, or nonhuman creatures. An example is, "The computer program has infinite patience." Obviously, a computer program cannot have "infinite patience," but by giving it this human quality, a speaker whose audience is novice users of the program makes a point about the program's ease of use.

Personification may also be used to set a general mood. Consider the effect of an opening narrative that begins with these words, "It was a dark and gloomy winter's day, with stubborn clouds threatening us every moment. . . ." You might expect suspense, mystery, or intrigue of some sort to follow. Part of the mood is created by the words *stubborn* and *threatening*. Since these are qualities of human beings, and not of clouds, attributing them to clouds gives greater liveliness to a speech.

Making Limited Use of Hyperbole

Hyperbole is perhaps the most commonly used figure of speech in everyday conversation. It consists of intentionally exaggerating in order to emphasize a point. Because most of us engage in hyperbole so regularly, much of our everyday use of it has become subconscious. Ordinarily, we are exaggerating subconsciously when using common expressions such as:

- She's the greatest!
- I've received truckloads of documents about our depreciation problem.
- The boss has gone ballistic on the Maxwell account!
- I'll give your company 110 percent.

Such statements are rarely true, of course, but the listener understands that the exaggeration is only intended to underscore the speaker's feelings.

In public speaking, hyperbole must be used sparingly, since in emphasizing too many points, a speaker winds up emphasizing none.

Understanding Understatement

Understatement is the opposite of hyperbole. Its purpose is to highlight something by playing down its importance or making what is significant sound insignificant. As an example, if a multimillionaire is asked about the extent of her wealth, she might use understatement in her reply, "Let's just say I'm not terribly worried about where my next meal is coming from."

Using Irony

Irony is a figure of speech in which the literal meaning expressed by a person's words is the opposite of the intended meaning. If you wished to show your dislike and lack of respect for another person, you might exclaim, "Oh, she's a fine person!" with a sarcastic tone in your voice that indicates you mean to convey the opposite of *fine*.

AVOIDING COMMON PROBLEMS

While language can be a public speaker's greatest asset, it can also trap a speaker into saying what is not meant or meaning what is not said. Following are several problems encountered in choosing effective language. A couple of these should always be avoided. Others may prove helpful or harmful, depending on how you use them.

Avoiding Unintentional Connotations

All words have a standard dictionary meaning. This is a generally accepted, objective meaning known as a word's denotation. Words may also have connotations, which are suggested or implied meanings for different people or different groups of people. If, for instance, a speaker were to use the word *gold,* the denotation would be "a heavy yellow metal." For some audience members, however, the connotation might include ideas of wealth or beauty. Speakers must be aware of the possible connotations the words they use are likely to carry for the bulk of their audiences. If the connotations are likely to cause strong negative reactions, it is wiser to choose other words.

Using Euphemisms Sparingly

Euphemisms are gentle or softened expressions for harsh or unpleasant realities. For example, people often say, "He passed on," as a gentler way of saying, "He died." Euphemisms are often helpful, since they allow a speaker to be tactful and avoid insulting an audience. Avoid using them so frequently that your message becomes clouded with soft terms, however.

Using Clichés at Your Own Risk

Clichés (like the one in the above heading) are expressions that at one time expressed a truth or idea clearly and briefly but have become so overused as to be almost meaningless. Examples of clichés are: "A stitch in time saves nine," "Where there's smoke, there's fire," "Green with envy," and "Pretty as a picture." The use of clichés generally bores an audience. It also causes listeners to lose a certain degree of respect for the speaker, since using clichés makes it appear that the speaker lacks originality.

Avoiding Stereotyping

Stereotyping means assigning qualities to people or objects because they are part of a general group, without considering their individual differences. Stereotypes may be based on a person's appearance, type of employment, nationality, religion, race, or age. "All bus drivers are rude" and "Young people are lazy" are examples of stereotyping. Using words or phrases that stereotype greatly harms a speaker's image. As such, they should always be avoided.

Using Slang Carefully

Slang consists of contemporary words and phrases that come in and go out of style very rapidly. Because the majority of slang expressions have a short life, using them in your speeches will confuse listeners who have never had a chance to become familiar with them. Some years ago, *cool* and *groovy* were "in" words. Today, the person who uses them sounds neither cool nor groovy. You should also remember that many slang expressions current among young people never get picked up by older people at all.

Be very thrifty in your use of slang even in conversation. You may wish to use it once in a while to produce an informal atmosphere or for novelty or humor, but beware of using it often in public speaking. As you gain more and more exposure to various types of speeches, notice how little slang good speakers use even in speeches delivered at very informal occasions. Slang dates your speech and, if overused, shows a limited vocabulary.

Avoiding Incorrect Grammar

Remember, words are the garments with which speakers clothe their ideas. If you use incorrect grammar, it is like appearing in public with your skirt on backwards or wearing socks that don't match. It is true that spoken language is often less formal than written language, but that does not mean it should be incorrect. The speaker heard saying, "All of us in this room has a stake in this problem," stands out like a person with shoes on the wrong feet. When the voice from the podium announces, "He laid down for a nap," listeners feel as they would when looking at someone with green hair. Granted, we all make grammatical slips from time to time. But the speaker who habitually does so loses the respect of his or her listeners. The chart in Exhibit 3.2 lists some of the common problem areas in grammar, along with their grammatical explanations and the correct usage for each.

As we close, keep in mind that errors in grammar may be repeated so often that they sound correct even when they are not. Practice proper usage until it sounds right to you.

EXHIBIT 3.2   Common Problem Areas in Grammatical Usage

Problem Area	Grammatical Explanation	Correct Usage
affect/effect	*affect* is usually a verb	That mistake may significantly *affect* your career.
	effect is generally a noun	The movie had quite an *effect* on me.
beside/besides	*beside* means "next to"	John stands *beside* Mary.
	besides means "in addition"	I don't like him; *besides,* he squints.
between you and I	the object of the preposition between is *me*	*between* you and me
can/may	*can* means "is able to"	He *can* win this race.
	may means "is allowed to"	She *may* go to the head of the line.
could care less	should be "couldn't care less" to state that someone was unconcerned	John *couldn't* care less about Paul's illness.
farther/further	use *farther* for real physical distance;	Cincinnati is *farther* than Louisville.
	use *further* for other kinds of distance	Nothing could be *further* from her mind.
irregardless/ regardless	always use r*egardless*	*Regardless* of the consequences, I am going ahead.
like	should not be used as a filler word, as in "He was, like, fifteen years old."	He was fifteen years old.
like/as if	do not use *like* in place of *as if*	You look as if (not *like*) you are thirsty.
that/which/who	*who* refers to people; *which* and *that* refer to things that are not people	I am the one *who* called. My car, *which* is ancient, won't start. I have a parrot *that* talks.

CHAPTER FOUR

Delivering the Speech: Using Your Voice and Your Body

Delivering a speech is not the same as delivering the mail or a loaf of bread. Generally, the mail and the bread are neither improved nor harmed during the process of being delivered to their destination. A speech or presentation, on the other hand, can be made much better or much worse by the manner in which it is delivered. Although delivery is not the most essential part of giving a speech, it is nonetheless very important. In short, good delivery can make a weak speech seem a bit better, while poor delivery can ruin an otherwise excellent speech.

In this chapter, we will discuss using your voice and body to improve your speech or presentation. The chapter will begin by defining and comparing several different methods of speech delivery before moving on to talk in detail about using your voice effectively—topics such as speaking with the right volume and using crisp articulation. Next comes a section on some of the specific nonverbal aspects of speech delivery, ranging from making eye contact to using notes effectively, and the use of visual aids, an all-important but often-neglected part of giving a speech or presentation. The final section will address some special challenges of delivering a speech, namely using the speaker's stand, handling the microphone, and dealing with distractions and interruptions.

UNDERSTANDING THE DIFFERENT METHODS OF SPEECH DELIVERY

Over the years, four basic methods for delivering public speeches have developed. One is called the manuscript method. Using this method, speakers write down everything they plan to say to their listeners, then bring their manuscripts to the podium and read them to the audience. A second method, called the memorization method, also begins with a written manuscript but differs in that the manuscript is memorized word-for-word and not used during delivery. Using a third method, the extemporaneous method, speakers prepare outlines of the ideas of their speeches beforehand but do not memorize an exact pattern of words. In short, they choose the words with which to clothe their ideas as they are speaking. As we discussed in Chapter 2, outlines or note cards may or may not be used. The fourth method, called the impromptu method, is used on occasions when people must speak "off the cuff," with no chance for previous preparation. This method demands that the speakers both organize their ideas and choose their words as they proceed through their speeches.

Comparing Methods of Delivery

Each of the four methods outlined above has advantages and disadvantages. One advantage of the manuscript method is that there is no danger of forgetting a part of your speech. Unless a sudden wind blows away your manuscript, about the worst thing that can happen is momentarily losing your place while reading. The manuscript method also allows you plenty of time beforehand to choose the most effective language for your speech. CEOs and other heads of companies often read from manuscripts when making major announcements or policy statements. This helps ensure that they do not make any "slips of the tongue" that could result in misunderstandings. A second advantage of the manuscript method is that speeches read from a manuscript often sound smoother than those delivered extemporaneously. The use of a manuscript also ensures precise timing of a speech, a factor of great importance for televised speeches, for instance.

On the other hand, many speeches read from manuscript *sound* as if they are being read. The audience is aware of the manuscript, and it prevents the speech from sounding natural. How many times have you had to listen to a speaker read from manuscript and felt like screaming at the speaker, "Stop reading *at* us and start talking *to* us"?

Memorized delivery has some of the same advantages as manuscript delivery. For instance, you may choose the most effective language beforehand, and your speech may be timed precisely. Memorized delivery often sounds prepackaged, however, as indeed it is. Word-for-word memorization also puts a tremendous burden on your memory for any speech longer than four or five minutes. This method of delivery is rarely used nowadays.

The major advantage of the extemporaneous method is that it sounds natural—much like ordinary conversation. Imagine for a moment that you and a close friend are planning to attend a big basketball game. At the last minute, your friend is prevented from going, so she asks you to tell her all about the game later. How would you go about preparing your "speech" for your friend? You could make a strong effort to remember all the important plays, the score, the poor calls by the referees (you might even take a few notes to remember), but you definitely wouldn't write out your description of the game word-for-word and later read it (or speak it by rote memory) to your friend. She would get bored listening to you "reading" about the game instead of "telling" her about it. Similarly, extemporaneous speaking sounds more like telling your speech to your audience than like reading it. No audience likes a speaker to read a message that can be told. Listeners will usually become bored and lose interest, even if the reader reads well. However, they are very tolerant of a speaker who looks them in the eye and addresses them directly, even if the flow of words is a bit halting.

The extemporaneous method also gives you the best opportunity to make use of positive and negative feedback from your audience. By constantly monitoring your listeners' reactions and making the necessary adjustments, you will improve your chances of maintaining a high level of audience interest and enthusiasm. Since the manuscript and memorization methods prevent this, they fall far short of the extemporaneous method of speaking in most instances.

Finally, the only advantage of impromptu delivery is that it sounds natural—much like ordinary conversation. Its major drawback, of course, is its tendency to sound unprepared. Unless a speaker has had considerable experience at impromptu speaking, this kind of delivery is likely to sound jumbled and awkward.

Combining Methods of Delivery

Of the four methods we have compared, extemporaneous delivery appears to have the greatest number of advantages. Many of the best speakers, however, find they are most effective when they combine methods. One of America's greatest public speakers, President Franklin D. Roosevelt, often prepared manuscripts for his major addresses and then regularly departed from them during delivery, speaking extemporaneously instead. Although this practice annoyed newspaper owners who had sometimes already printed the advance text in their papers, it was extremely effective with Roosevelt's audiences. By combining the methods in this way, he was able to gain the advantages of each, while avoiding their pitfalls.

Combining methods of delivery requires a certain degree of skill and experience because you don't want your listeners to be able to detect which parts are being read from manuscript, which are memorized, and which are being spoken extemporaneously. Combining methods effectively also requires skill in the use of the extemporaneous method, since the extemporaneous parts must sound as fluent and well prepared as the manuscript sections. However, you can begin to use a combination of methods in small ways.

To become practiced at using a combination of methods, begin by memorizing your introductory remarks and your conclusion. A memorized introduction gets you off to a smooth start, sounds impressive, and helps build your confidence for the body of the speech. Similarly, a carefully worded and memorized conclusion can make a lasting impression on the audience and end your speech effectively. Major transition sentences within the body of the speech may also be memorized. The manuscript method may be used for brief sections of the body where you wish to insert a direct quotation in the original author's language or present a set of statistics too complex to memorize. This kind of material can be written out fully on note cards or a manuscript page and read at appropriate points in your speech. Most of the body of the speech can then be prepared using the extemporaneous method.

As a final note, beware of preparing lengthy sections of your early speeches by the manuscript or memorization methods. Remember that your main concentration should be on perfecting the extemporaneous method, since it will serve as the backbone for any combination of methods you may wish to use later.

MASTERING THE VOCAL ASPECTS OF SPEECH DELIVERY

A large part of the message of a speech is, of course, carried by the voice— what the audience *hears*. How you control and use your voice, coupled with the words you choose, can make the difference between a well received and a poorly received speech. There are several factors of voice usage to keep in mind when you are delivering a speech, including speaking with the right volume, varying your pitch, watching your speaking rate, using crisp articulation and correct pronunciation, and pausing effectively.

Speaking with the Right Volume

No matter how well organized, researched, and rehearsed a speech may be, if the listeners cannot hear what is being said, the speech cannot possibly succeed. Although it is possible to speak too loudly for a given room or audience, most beginning speakers have the opposite problem: they speak too softly and cannot be heard in the rear of the room. This may be due in some part to nervousness, but more often inexperienced speakers simply do not realize they are not using sufficient volume.

Volume is controlled primarily by the amount of air a person forces through the vocal cords. By inhaling, you obtain a supply of air in your lungs that can then be used to produce vocal tones (sounds) by forcing the air across your vocal cords as you exhale. Therefore, if you are going to speak very loudly, you must have a considerable supply of air in your lungs. And if you need to speak loudly for an extended period of time (as in a public speech), you need a constant, large supply of air.

Research has found that people use sixty-six times as much energy addressing a large audience in a large room as they do in ordinary conversation, so the manner in which you inhale while speaking becomes very important. Inhale deeply through your nose, sucking in air by expanding your diaphragm (the area between your chest and stomach). Upper-chest breathing by itself does not provide enough air for an extended sentence in a large auditorium, but diaphragmatic breathing provides plenty. Besides, filling the lower lungs with air does not really take much longer than shallow inhalation.

How you exhale is also important in sustaining sufficient volume. If you let all the air out as you say your first few words, one of two problems will occur: either the ends of your longer sentences will be too soft to be heard, or you will need to inhale so often you will begin to sound like an air compressor at work. As you gain experience in public speaking, you will learn to pace your exhalation, saving enough air for emphasizing important ideas with extra force.

Variety in volume is important, too. A speaker who is constantly loud makes everything sound important. The net effect on the audience is that eventually nothing sounds important. Conversely, when the audience has to strain constantly to hear someone who is speaking softly, they eventually give up and stop listening. It is best to take a middle ground. Always convey important or key ideas with sufficient force so that those in the back row can hear them easily. Transitions to new sections of a speech, the start of the conclusion, and the parts where you wish to be dramatic with a kind of "stage whisper" may be spoken more softly but should still be audible for listeners in the rear of the room.

Varying Your Pitch

Pitch refers to the tone of the voice on the musical scale. Words or syllables to be emphasized are usually spoken in a higher pitch, or key, while strong emotion is generally indicated by great differences in pitch among words or syllables that are used together. Think, for example, of the many ways in which you might pronounce the following sentence: "I certainly don't think that!"

Changing pitch as you speak comes naturally to you in conversation, but beginning public speakers often fail to maintain their pitch variety when speaking from a public platform. Speaking in a monotone, with no ups or downs in pitch, can quickly give an audience the impression that the speaker is not enthusiastic or sincere about the topic. Of course, pitch changes should not be affected. The enthusiasm must first be present. Then pitch variety will naturally follow.

Each of us has a general pitch—that portion of your range in which your voice usually hovers when you speak. For public speaking, each person needs to discover his or her optimum pitch within that range—the pitch that can be used most comfortably without strain for extended periods of time. The most comfortable tones are found most often in the lower half of a person's range.

Watching Your Speaking Rate

One's typical speaking rate varies from about 120 to 150 words per minute, although some people regularly speak more rapidly or more slowly than others, and nearly everyone varies his or her speaking rate for different situations.

Inexperienced speakers often speak too rapidly due to nervousness. If you find you are speaking too rapidly, force yourself to slow down by concentrating on the problem. Changes in rate are brought about in two ways:

by varying the number and length of pauses between words or by varying the length of time it takes to pronounce each syllable. If you are told that you are speaking too rapidly, the best place to begin a correction is with your pauses. A well-timed pause supported by appropriate gestures, movement, and eye contact can often say much more than several sentences. You do not have to emit some kind of sound every second you are before an audience—learn to pause for several seconds between major segments of your speech and more briefly between sentences.

A specific problem common to many speakers is called the vocalized pause. This is the habit of filling in pauses with *uh, er, um,* or similar nonmeaningful sounds. If these sounds become too numerous, they can be very distracting to your listeners. Here are two methods for handling the vocalized pause:

1. Make a list of transition words to use between sentences and vary them regularly during your speech.

2. Rehearse your speeches with a tape recorder and listen to yourself. Hearing a great number of vocalized pauses in one's own speech can often motivate a person to concentrate seriously on solving the problem.

Using Crisp Articulation and Correct Pronunciation

"Watcha doin ta-day, Sam?" "I dunno. Wudder you?" This kind of talk may communicate minimally in informal conversation with friends, but it would brand a public speaker as unprofessional and wholly inarticulate. Articulation refers to the way in which the tongue, teeth, palate, and lips are moved and used to produce the crisp, clear sounds of good speech. Most people are capable of producing vowel and consonant sounds clearly but fall into lazy habits. They become unwilling to exert that extra bit of effort needed to produce clear speech. Unfortunately, when a speaker carries such bad habits into public speaking, an audience may show little respect; they will hear a speaker who sounds sloppy or mushy and interpret the information being conveyed as sloppy or mushy, too.

To ensure clear articulation in your speeches and presentations, rehearse it. Concentrate on moving your tongue, lips, and lower jaw vigorously enough to produce crisp, clear sounds as you practice your speech. Be especially careful with consonants that are easily slurred or dropped altogether. Don't use "madder" when you mean "matter" or "gonna" for "going to," for instance.

Pronunciation can also play a role in determining the degree of respect the audience gives a speaker. Pronunciation involves selecting the correct sounds and the proper syllable stresses. What makes a certain pronunciation correct and another incorrect is usage. That is, once enough people agree to pronounce a word in a certain way, it becomes the correct way by default. But you cannot assume that your friends, or even all the people in your organization, have cornered the market on correct pronunciation. The two best sources for discovering the accepted pronunciation of words are the dictionary and the prominent speakers of the day, such as national news commentators and noted government officials.

If you need to use proper names or technical terms in a speech, be certain you know the accepted pronunciation before beginning your rehearsal. Using the correct sounds and stresses during rehearsal will usually ensure correct pronunciation during the live performance. When you pronounce unusual words with authority and without hesitation, your audience is likely to be impressed by the thoroughness of your speech preparation and feel you have genuinely earned the right to speak to them.

Pausing Effectively

Beginning speakers often have difficulty pausing effectively. Some rush ahead like a speeding rocket with no pauses at all; others fill their pauses with meaningless sounds like *uh, er,* and *um;* still others pause in the middle of thoughts rather than at the end.

As you become aware of and correct pausing problems, you will also want to discover ways to make pausing work for you to improve your speech rather than detract from it. The well-known American writer Mark Twain, who gave many speeches during his life, once said, "The right word may be effective, but no word was ever as effective as a rightly timed pause." Especially in speeches to entertain, a pause of just the right length in just the right place can result in more thunderous laughter than a lengthy story.

There is no quick way to learn how to pause effectively in public speaking—it is mostly a matter of timing and comes primarily from experience—but here are a few pointers:

- When you listen to experienced speakers, notice when they pause and for how long. Pay attention to their audiences' reactions.

- Practice pausing when rehearsing your own speeches.

- Use pauses when you wish to create a dramatic effect, when you want to signal to your listeners that you are changing thoughts, or when you wish to create laughter.

- Be aware that what usually seems like a three-minute pause to a beginning speaker is actually about three seconds in length.

- When pausing for laughter or applause from your audience, do not continue with your speech until the listeners' reactions have subsided; however, you should begin speaking again before all the applause or laughter has died down lest you lose momentum or create the impression that you wanted more recognition than you received.

PRACTICING NONVERBAL ASPECTS OF SPEECH DELIVERY

Dr. Ray Birdwhistell, one of the foremost scholars in nonverbal communication, claims that words account for only 35 percent of what we communicate; the remainder is largely accomplished by body motion. Although the figure may be exaggerated, it emphasizes an important concept for public speakers: You can accomplish communication through what the audience *sees,* as well as through what the audience *hears.* Eye contact, gestures, platform movement, appearance, and the motions you make as you begin and end a speech will "say" a great deal about you and your message to the listeners.

Beginning Your Speech

You may think that your speech begins when you speak the first word. In truth, however, the audience starts making judgments about you from the moment you rise from your seat to approach the speaker's platform. You nonverbally communicate self-confidence, poise, and leadership, or nervousness, disorganization, and timidity simply by the manner in which you approach the platform or presentation area and take command of it.

Walk to the platform vigorously but not hastily. Arrange any notes you might have on the lectern. Turn your face up toward your listeners and look about at various sides of the audience for several seconds before you begin to speak. An unhurried beginning assures your audience of your confidence and command of the situation.

Making Eye Contact

As you speak, establish eye contact with your listeners. Look directly into the eyes of various audience members. This causes most listeners to feel as if you are devoting your attention to them personally in the same way you would if you were conversing with them individually. The greater the proportion of your speaking time you devote to eye contact, the deeper and more positive this impression becomes.

Looking at your listeners also performs a second important function: It makes it possible for you to monitor the feedback. Feedback is simply the total of all visible and audible reactions of the audience to the speaker. It can consist of yawns, smiles, boos, hisses, questioning looks, applause, and even fidgeting in the seats. When you use extemporaneous delivery, you are largely free to read your listeners' feedback and then adjust your approach to maintain positive feedback.

When making eye contact, look at one audience member for several seconds as you speak, then turn your head slightly to look at another. Don't forget the people at the sides of the room near the front. Because speakers must turn their heads farther to look at them, these listeners are often cheated out of eye contact.

Some beginning speakers report that looking directly at their listeners makes then nervous and confused. If this happens to you, you may wish to look at your audience as a whole for awhile rather than directly into individuals' eyes. Beware of getting into a habit of doing this, however. Eye contact is so important for both speaker and audience that its absence can sometimes ruin an otherwise good speech. Once you have gained some experience and have learned to relax on the platform, you should be able to maintain real eye contact without difficulty.

Using Gestures

Communicating nonverbally through gestures is a natural part of human communication, yet many beginning speakers become stiff as a board when they give a speech. Nevertheless, because we all gesture naturally, the urge to gesture will ordinarily return once a speaker has gained platform experience. Gestures fall into two general categories: arm-hand and head-facial.

ARM AND HAND GESTURES. Most arm and hand gestures fall into one of four types. Emphatic gestures help the speaker stress what he or she is saying. These include making a fist, raising one hand with the palm up, and pointing with the index finger at the audience when saying something such as, "It's your responsibility. . . ." Transitional gestures show that you are moving from one part of your speech to another. They include using your fingers to enumerate points, placing both palms on the podium, and moving both hands, with palms facing each other, from one side to the other in front of you. When a speaker uses descriptive gestures, he or she moves the hands and arms to draw pictures in the air. These may indicate the size of an object, such as "the fish that got away," or the general shape of something. Finally, locative gestures direct the listeners' attention to some place, object, or person. They are usually made with the index finger or with the entire hand.

Books on public speaking used to include long lists and extensive illustrations of gestures, showing in detail how they should be made. The problem with that approach was that it was like telling a speaker which words to use. In reality, each person has her or his own style of nonverbal communication—just as each chooses his or her own words. When you gesture during a speech or presentation, it should be because it feels natural in that moment. If, for instance, you are describing a distant place and it seems appropriate to extend your arm to indicate great distance, then by all means extend your arm. If you refer to that same distant place later in the same speech and this time it does not seem appropriate to extend your arm, then don't. Good gestures are basically a matter of what feels appropriate at the moment, without any lengthy thought about it.

Although it is helpful for beginning speakers to make some gestures while speaking, it is not good to force gestures. Certainly it is not wise to decide during a prespeech rehearsal that you are definitely going to make a particular gesture at a specific point in your speech. Preconceived gestures usually look rehearsed if made during the live speech.

Speakers sometimes ask, "What should I do with my arms and hands when I am not using them to gesture?" Unfortunately, no single answer can be given. As with gestures, basic hand and arm positions must be natural to you, as well as suited to the audience and the total speaking situation. Here are some commonly used positions that you may want to consider:

- One or both arms hanging naturally at your sides.
- One or both hands resting on (not grasping) the speaker's stand.
- One or both hands being held about at waist level.

These positions will look quite natural for some speakers but not for others. Over time, you can learn from the reactions of your audiences which positions suit you best. When you have a friend in the audience, gather up your courage following the speech and ask the friend for an honest critique of your gesturing.

HEAD AND FACIAL GESTURES. Audience members ordinarily pay more attention to a speaker's head and facial gestures than they do to arm or hand movements. Smiles, frowns, nods, and any other movements of the head, eyebrows, chin, lips, or forehead can create an impression of a dynamic and enthusiastic speaker, as long as they are appropriate to the spoken message. As with any gesture, head and facial movements must be natural. They must come from your inner enthusiasm about your message and not be practiced or tacked on for show.

Many beginning speakers show too somber a face to their audiences. Of course, some topics demand a serious countenance, but many do not. A speaker laying out "techniques for presiding over business meetings," for instance, need not look overly solemn to the listeners. Instead, a generally pleasant look, altered at times when the topic turns serious, shows the listeners an appropriate variety in facial expression. Essentially, a speaker's face should portray the thoughts and emotions he or she is speaking about at any given moment in a speech. If a speaker is enthusiastic about and involved in the topic, facial expression will follow as naturally as water seeking its own level. The spoken message will flow over into complementary facial gestures as well as numerous other forms of nonverbal communication.

VARYING YOUR GESTURES. It bears repeating that variety is the spice of public speaking, just as it is of life. Like all other parts of a speech, gestures (whether arm-hand or head-facial) must be varied regularly to maintain audience attention and interest. A speaker who makes the same gesture repeatedly distracts the audience with that gesture. Pretty soon many listeners will be wondering when the gesture will occur again and will be paying little attention to the message. While some particularly famous speakers can get away with overworked gestures, because they have so many other outstanding qualities as speakers, unknown speakers must be doubly careful of any gesture that becomes a regular pattern in their speeches. While taking care not to overuse any one gesture, remember that using no gestures at all is just as deadly. In addition, a speaker's face should be expressive. Facial gestures such as raising the eyebrows, smiling, frowning, and widening the eyes indicate your involvement with your topic and generate interest and enthusiasm in your audience.

Using Platform Movement

The way in which a speaker uses movements involving the entire body (known as platform movement but not necessarily limited to being on a platform) can also project a certain image to the audience. The question here is, "How can one make the best use of positive forms of movement?" Like gestures, platform movement should look and feel natural. The best way to achieve this is to move when there is a reason to move and to remain still otherwise. Legitimate reasons to move during a speech are similar to reasons for moving during a one-to-one conversation. Ask yourself, "When do I ordinarily move about when I'm having a conversation with a friend?" Your answers are likely to include at least two or three of the following reasons:

- To whisper something confidential or intimate to the other person.
- To compensate when the listener shifts his or her position.
- To change to a new topic or to change the mood.
- To provide variety.

Reasons for platform movement during a speech fall into the same categories. You may want to get closer to the audience to show greater confidentiality or intimacy, to compensate for audience members' fidgeting in their seats, to emphasize a change to a new topic or section of your speech at major transition points, or to create a bit of visual variety.

As a final note, platform movement looks best when it is made on a diagonal—not directly on a forward-backward axis nor completely on a side-to-side axis but somewhere in between the two.

Using Notes Effectively

Speaking extemporaneously means having your pattern of ideas clearly in mind as you begin your speech but selecting your words spontaneously. Many extemporaneous speakers use note cards to ensure that they do not forget a major point or to read an occasional direct quote or set of statistics. You have probably seen speakers who used note cards so effectively that you were barely aware the speakers had them. Conversely, you have also probably suffered through speeches in which the speaker fumbled the note cards, held the note cards out at arm's length to read them, or otherwise distracted you with them. Observing these few tips on the preparation and use of note cards can make all the difference in whether they enhance or detract from your speech or presentation:

- Cards containing your outline should be very brief. Use only a word or short phrase to remind you of each point in your speech.

- Cards containing direct quotes or sets of statistics should contain only one item of information each and should be arranged in the proper order before the speech begins. Be certain you write your source of information at the top of the cards.

- Write or type in large, bold characters so that each card can be easily read from the podium (or from a comfortable distance if you are not using a podium).

- Place the cards near the top edge of the podium so the audience doesn't think you're looking at your feet when you're glancing at your cards.

- Feel free to hold one or more cards in your hand if you move away from the podium, but use only 3" x 5" cards if you do this.

- Plan not to look at your outline card at all during your presentation. It should be there only as a comforting refuge should you forget a point.

Making the Most of Your Appearance

Much of the appeal of glamorous stars comes from their appearance—the carefully styled hair, the beautiful gowns, the glittering jewels. Speakers, too, are often judged as much by how they look as by what they have to say. A speaker's overall appearance should be suited to his or her personality, the audience being addressed, and the occasion for which the speech is being given.

The most obvious measure of appearance is the clothing you wear. Your clothing says a great deal about your attitude toward your listeners and how much importance you attach to the speech itself. Speakers who radically violate the audience's expectations concerning clothing and general appearance have two strikes against them before they say their first sentence. You can improve your chances of creating a good impression by asking yourself, "What is the most appropriate clothing to wear for this particular audience and set of circumstances?"

More important than appropriate clothing, however, is a speaker's overall look. Whereas clothing might vary according to your personality, the audience, or the occasion, neatness is *always* necessary when you are giving a speech or presentation. Even when the most informal mode of dress is called for, neat and clean clothes—together with clean hair, fingernails, face, and hands—are a must. A sloppy appearance automatically communicates to your audience, "I'm not interested in giving this speech, so I didn't spend much time getting ready to speak to you." Clearly, there is no benefit to be gained from sending this kind of message to an audience. On the other hand, by making the most of your appearance, you demonstrate respect for yourself and esteem for your audience.

Concluding Your Speech

Just as the speech begins at the moment you rise from your seat, it does not conclude until you have retaken your seat. As such, an unhurried departure is essential. You do not want to create the impression that you wish to leave the platform as quickly as possible. Once you have spoken your final word, pause momentarily while still facing the audience to let the impact of your conclusion sink in, and then walk to your seat in a manner appropriate to your topic. If your speech was serious in nature, a grave and solemn return is suggested. If the topic was light or entertaining, a more cheerful mode is appropriate. Above all, do not ruin the effect of a good presentation by showing you felt you spoke poorly as you depart from the platform. Let the audience be the judge of that.

Using Visual Aids

Visual aids are very helpful for both the speaker and the listeners, especially during informative speaking and demonstrations. For the speaker, they provide a natural excuse to move about on the platform, to gesture, and to point. They can also help the speaker remember details of the presentation. Members of the audience find that visual aids deepen their perception and understanding of the speaker's message and help them remember the details of the speech.

While well-used visual aids can improve a speech in a number of ways, they can also turn a speech into a disaster if a speaker attempts to use them without thorough preparation and practice. Because speaking with visual aids involves doing two things at once—maintaining the verbal flow and handling physical objects—it is never easy. As a result, more careful preparation is called for when you are readying a speech that involves visual aids than for a speech without. You must consider such issues as when to use visuals, what types of aids to use, and what equipment is involved.

Deciding When to Use Visuals

How do you know when to include visual aids in a speech? Ask yourself these two questions: "If I use a certain visual, will its presence make it easier for me to get my point across?" and "Will using a certain visual make the point more meaningful for my audience?" If the answer to either question seems to be yes, then you should include the visual. Suppose, for example, you need to provide a training session for new employees on how to operate a fax machine. Your training session would be far more difficult to present and far less informative for your new employees if no fax machine were present. Yes, you could train the group without the machine, but the session would likely prove notably longer, and less learning would occur as well.

Once you have decided to use visual aids in a speech, beware of the temptation to overuse them. Visual aids in speeches should always remain in the role their name implies: aids. Once they become the main focus of audience interest and attention, they have ceased to be aids and have turned a speech into a presentation of the visuals themselves. Using five or six of your best slides, for example, would likely enhance your speech, but showing twenty-five or thirty slides during a short presentation means you are no longer giving a speech with visual aids; you are giving a slide show with a brief commentary.

Choosing the Appropriate Type of Visual Aids

For some speeches you may want to use several types of visual aids, while for others only one will be necessary. The type and number depend on your speech topic and the relationship of the visual aids to it. Following are brief descriptions of some of the kinds of visual aids that are available to a speaker. Be aware, however, that the visual aids mentioned here are not the only types of visual aids available; they are simply the ones most commonly used. Anything that can visually support a speech and is appropriate for the speaker, audience, and occasion may be used as a visual aid.

CHARTS. A chart is a drawing showing the relationships among the parts of a whole. The drawing usually includes lines and words and can deal with almost any subject. One commonly used type of chart is the organizational chart, which shows the relationships among members of an organization (see Exhibit 4.1).

GRAPHS. A second common type of visual aid is the graph. Graphs picture large amounts of information (usually quantitative) at a single glance. One frequently used type is the line graph, which consists primarily of lines with occasional words and numbers. When the area under the peaks and valleys on a line graph is darkened to provide greater visual contrast, the graph is called a profile graph. Other types of graphs include bar, circle or pie (shown in Exhibit 4.2), and picture graphs.

DIAGRAMS. Like a chart or a graph, a diagram is used to show the relationship of a part to a whole. Diagrams, however, generally rely more on draw-

EXHIBIT 4.1   Sample Organizational Chart

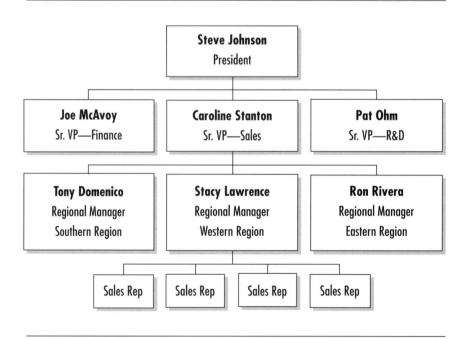

ing and less on words and numbers than charts and graphs do. Diagrams may range from very simple line drawings to very complex pictures with shading and perspective.

Maps. A map shows information that is geographical in nature. Some maps are used simply to indicate location; others show location as it relates to elevation, weather, agricultural production, or any number of other factors.

Posters. A relatively easy type of visual aid to prepare is one consisting of print or lettering on a poster. Lists of important points in your speech, key phrases, slogans, and humorous sayings can all be visually presented through print. Simply printing the main ideas of a speech on a large sheet of paper and showing it to the audience does not make an effective visual aid, however. Printed visual aids should be genuinely attention-getting or essential memory aids. The lettering must be imaginative, with attention given to spacing, color, size of letters, and font style. A sample of a possible poster for a speech on copyright law is shown in Exhibit 4.3.

EXHIBIT 4.2   Sample Bar Graph

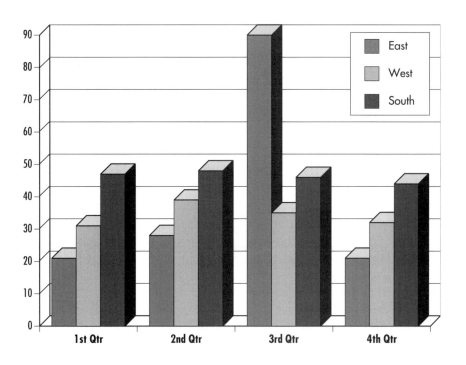

EXHIBIT 4.3   Sample Poster

TODAY'S AGENDA

Welcome and Introductions	9:00-9:30
Overview of Copyright Law	9:30-11:00
Copyright of Nonprint Media	11:00-12:00
Lunch	12:00

CARTOONS. Cartoons turn humor into a visual aid. A cartoon is simply a funny or satirical drawing used to make a point. Although cartoons demand a certain artistic ability to be effective, their impact on an audience can be great when they are well prepared.

PICTURES. Whether simply printed or presented by means of photograph, slide, film, or via multimedia presentation, a picture can be a very effective visual aid. However, two cautions must be observed when using pictures. First, they must be large enough to be easily seen by the entire audience. If necessary, pictures must be enlarged to assure that even those in the back row of a large hall can see everything clearly and easily. Second, pictures must be used sparingly because they can easily become the center of attention and distract the audience from the speaker and the message. When these cautions are observed, a picture can, indeed, be worth a thousand words.

OBJECTS. A three-dimensional object will often make a deeper impression with an audience than a two-dimensional picture or representation. Imagine an auctioneer showing pictures of the items for sale versus holding up the real objects as he or she talks.

Sometimes an object is too large to be conveniently brought to a speech presentation. In such a case, a scaled-down version, called a model, may be used instead. A plastic model of a rocket, for example, enables the speaker to show parts and views sometimes not possible with either a real rocket or a two-dimensional drawing. Models of many large objects may not be readily available, but often an inexpensive one can be made from cardboard or papier-mâché. Additionally, models with a section of the outer covering removed to show interior parts (called cutaways) can also be used. A model of a frog showing its musculature and internal organs would be an example of a cutaway.

HANDOUTS. Materials prepared ahead of time to give to each member of your audience are called handouts. They may contain outlines, explanations, directions, maps, charts, or other information that augments what you are presenting. Handouts are especially useful if you are presenting information to your audience that they will want to refer to after your speech is over. Be sure to have enough copies of your handouts available for every member of your audience.

Preparing Speeches Using Visual Aids

Because speeches containing visual aids are more difficult to deliver than speeches without, precise preparation and practice is called for when aids are to be used. As a rule, visual aids must be visible or legible to your entire audience, neat and attractive, well planned, and carefully rehearsed.

VISIBILITY. The first principle regarding the selection and preparation of any visual aid you plan to display is that it must be easily visible or legible from all parts of the room—even to the people in the back rows. Elementary as this may seem, it is one of the most frequently violated rules regarding the use of visual aids. The best way to ensure good visibility is to place your visual aid across a room of the approximate size in which the actual speech will be given and check for yourself.

Keep in mind as you prepare your visual aids that graphic visuals such as charts, graphs, diagrams, maps, cartoons, and posters should have large and heavily drawn letters, numbers, and lines, as well as sufficient contrast with the background on which they are mounted. Snapshots and pictures cut from newspapers or magazines are rarely large enough for even a small audience to see details without projection. Occasionally actual objects or models are even too small for easy viewing of details, as well. Remember, however, that the audience only needs to see whatever degree of detail you consider important. If minute details of the visual are not essential to your speech, then it is not necessary that they be large.

NEATNESS AND ATTRACTIVENESS. A second necessary element in visual aid preparation is that visual aids must be neat and attractive. This is not to say your visuals need to be works of art, but they should never be sloppy. One of the major problems with drawing a visual on a blackboard or easel while you are speaking is that, unless you are indeed an artist, it is difficult to produce a visual in a neat and attractive way under pressure. Preparing well-proportioned visuals ahead of time, on the other hand, can greatly enhance your prestige with your audience. It gives listeners the impression that you were concerned enough about the reception of your speech to take pains to create attractive visual aids.

Although the stress should be on neatness when you are preparing your visuals, don't overlook the opportunity to highlight important points through the use of various colors and media. Felt-tip pens, crayons, premade lettering, ink, and many other elements can be combined to produce a visual that is both informative and appealing. Nowadays, the use of personal computers with graphics programs provides nearly unlimited opportunities for creating professional visuals in a short period of time. Examples of sloppy and neat graphics are shown in Exhibit 4.4. Which would you rather present to your audience?

GOOD PLANNING. Prior to your speech or presentation, you will also need to plan how to display the visual aids. Small objects, models, and cutaways can be held in your hands and shown to the audience with relative ease. Most good graphic and pictorial aids, however, will be so large that holding them while speaking will look clumsy and awkward to the audience. If an easel is available, it can be very useful in displaying larger visuals—as long as you make sure it is placed at the proper angle to be seen from all parts of the room. When an easel is not available, you may want to bring masking tape to help you properly display the visual. In this case, be certain it is placed high enough so that the audience can see it. You should also make sure it is far enough from the lectern that your body will not block the listeners' views. Finally, if you decide to lean the visual against something—an easel, the lectern, or a blackboard—you must use cardboard that is heavy enough to remain in place without being held.

Keep in mind that you will need to point to various details on your visual at certain places in your speech. Because pointing with your hand often means your arm blocks part of your audience's view of the visual, you should use a pointer if at all possible. To use the pointer effectively, hold it in whichever hand is closer to the visual so you do not have to reach across your body to point. Then, with your pointer touching the visual, turn your eyes immediately back to your audience. If you will be pointing to the visual repeatedly, keep the pointer in your hands during that portion of your speech in which you are making frequent references to the aid. If, on the other hand, you plan to refer to the visual at only a few widely separated times during the speech, lay the pointer aside and pick it up again the next time it is needed.

Two other important matters to consider are the point at which you first wish to display a visual and the length of time you will want to continue to display it. If the aid will be referred to off and on throughout most

EXHIBIT 4.4   Clear and Neat Visual Aids: Which Would You Prefer to Use?

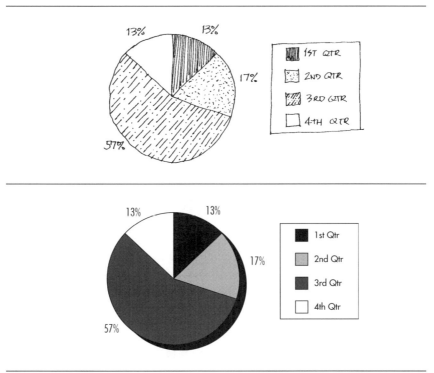

of the speech, you want to show it to the audience when you first make reference to it and then let it remain in view until the speech is completed. If the visual is to be referred to only once or for the final time well before the speech is completed, you should put it aside or cover it immediately after your last reference to it. Otherwise, it will distract the listeners by remaining in view. Visuals mounted on cardboard may be turned face down on a desk or table. Objects, models, and cutaways can sometimes be covered with a piece of cloth.

CAREFUL REHEARSAL. In order for a speech involving visual aids to look smooth and professional, you must practice coordinating the verbal and the visual elements. In your prespeech rehearsals, practice when first to display the visuals, how to display them, for what length of time, and when and how to remove them from view. Also, be certain that your body does not block the audience's view of the visual aids and that you are comfortable handling them—you don't want to risk dropping an object because you didn't realize how heavy it was!

A second important element of rehearsing visuals is achieving good timing with them. Some visuals are used to make a single point in a speech. If you plan to use one or more visual aids of this type, be certain to give the audience sufficient time to view it. Inexperienced speakers often work hard to produce a neat, attractive visual, then lose its effectiveness by displaying it for only two to three seconds. If the audience is to have only one opportunity to see a visual, they will ordinarily need about ten to twelve seconds to familiarize themselves with its content. It is perfectly acceptable to display an aid in silence for several seconds after explaining it to the audience.

Using Visual Aids in Demonstration Speeches

Many demonstration speeches—those which show your listeners how to do something, how to make something, or how something works—demand the use of visual aids. Each type of demonstration requires different procedures with visual aids.

To show your listeners how to perform a process themselves, arrange the steps in the process sequentially, demonstrating each step in order. For this form of demonstration speech, aids such as objects, models, and mockups usually prove more effective than graphs, charts, and diagrams. Don't overlook your own body as an effective visual aid, as well. A nurse training paramedics in proper techniques of drawing blood, for instance, will likely model the steps in the process with his or her hands. Also, keep the number of separate steps in the process to a minimum. If the process has more than five separate steps, try to group the steps into stages. This will aid the listeners' memories. Likewise, avoid handling too many separate aids. Use one, two, or three key aids to demonstrate the process.

When the purpose of your speech is to have your audience understand rather than learn to perform a process, you have greater choice in how you arrange the steps. Arrangements such as easy-to-difficult, order of importance, known-to-unknown, and chronological order may be used. To demonstrate three methods of thawing a frozen pipe, for example, you might use an order of most-preferred to least-preferred where the order is:

1. Heat the pipe with a torch (most-preferred method).

2. Pour boiling water over cloth wrapped around the pipe.

3. Wrap the pipe with electrical heat tape (least-preferred method).

Graphs, charts, and pictures may often be just as useful as objects and models when you want your listeners to understand a process. A picture or drawing of a torch heating a frozen pipe, for instance, should prove just as effective as (and easier to handle than) an actual torch.

As a final word, take care not to fall into the trap of allowing the "demonstration" part to steal the show when you are giving demonstration speeches. When this happens you are no longer giving a speech supported by a visual demonstration; you are giving a demonstration supported by a few remarks.

Using Visual Aids Equipment

Some visual aids can best be presented through the use of some form of equipment—a computer, an overhead projector, a videotape player, or a slide projector, to name a few. When equipment is to be used, rehearsing with the equipment is as crucial as rehearsing with the visual aids themselves. Most methods of projection require a darkened or semidarkened room, so you must be certain this can be arranged before choosing a visual requiring projection. Moreover, many times it is best to arrange for an assistant to run the equipment during your speech and to turn the lights on and off at the proper times to relieve you of having too many responsibilities all at once. Naturally, such preparations must all be rehearsed in advance.

On the day of the speech itself, carefully set up the equipment and check it prior to the speech. Don't assume that the computer program will run without a hitch, that the projector bulb is all right, or that the videotape player is working properly. Probably more good speeches have been ruined by burned-out bulbs than by any other single cause. Finally, it is wise to plan how you will handle the situation if a piece of equipment malfunctions during your presentation. Perhaps you can prepare handouts in advance to use in case other materials cannot be used, or it may be possible for you to explain verbally the material you had planned to display. In any event, remember that audiences are usually sympathetic, so don't panic!

ADDRESSING SPECIAL CHALLENGES OF DELIVERING A SPEECH

Delivering a speech sometimes involves dealing with special challenges and situations. Among these are the use of a speaker's stand and microphone and coping with distractions and interruptions. Practice at handling these matters can help you immeasurably when you encounter them in a live presentation.

Using the Speaker's Stand

In the majority of locations where you might give a speech or presentation, some type of speaker's stand, or lectern, will be available. Occasionally, however, you may encounter a situation in which a lectern is not available.

Therefore, a good speaker needs to know both how to use a speaker's stand effectively and how to get along without one.

The basic purpose of a lectern is to hold a speaker's notes or manuscript. It was never intended to serve as a support for speakers with weak backs or as a hiding place for those with wobbly knees. A person who uses the speaker's stand to lounge upon or to hide behind immediately reveals apathy or extreme nervousness to the audience. Occasionally allowing one or both hands to rest on the stand is acceptable—as long as you do not grasp the stand so desperately that your knuckles turn white! You should never place your foot on the base of the stand, either. Both feet should be flat on the floor behind the stand. In general, the less the lectern is grasped, leaned on, caressed, or tapped on, the better the overall impression will be.

Usually the top surface of a lectern is tilted at an angle to allow a speaker to read note cards or manuscript pages with ease, while at the same time keeping them out of sight. The best way to handle papers on a lectern is to lay them on the stand at the start and *leave them there throughout the speech*. The audience should be as unaware of your notes as possible, so you must avoid picking them up and putting them down or holding them in your hands. In addition, cards or manuscript pages should be brought to the lectern in a prearranged order. Try to avoid using paper clips or staples that will require removal or the flipping of pages. When the top card or page has been used, you need only to slide it gently and quietly to one side, exposing the next card or page. Picking up a stack of cards in order to place the used one on the bottom of the stack can be very distracting to the listeners, as is the flapping of stapled manuscript pages over the front of a speaker's stand.

If you want to use note cards but have no stand on which to place them, remember that the easiest size to hold is a 3" x 5" card. As each one is used, you can quietly slip it to the back of the deck, making the next card ready for reference. A full-sized manuscript is more difficult to handle without a speaker's stand. Thus, if you intend to read from manuscript, you should always find out whether or not a stand will be available. If a lectern will not be available, you can then transfer your speech onto 3" x 5" cards.

One advantage of having no lectern when you are using note cards is the additional freedom you have to move about on the platform. Not feeling tied to the stand allows you to walk a few steps more often, reducing your tension and generating greater audience attention.

Using a Microphone

When you are speaking to more than eighty people or are in a room where the acoustics are poor, you will find a microphone helpful. However, in order for a microphone to enhance the communication rather than harm it, it must be used properly. The number one rule in the proper use of a microphone is to test it before the speech begins if at all possible! Probably more speeches have gotten off to weak starts because of untested, faulty microphones than due to any other single cause. It only takes a moment to confirm that (1) the microphone is turned on, (2) there is no electronic feedback, and (3) it is set at the proper distance and height.

Just how far should the microphone be from the speaker's mouth? Microphones vary somewhat, but an average of ten to twelve inches works well for most microphones. Of course, you must keep this "mouth-to-mike" distance fairly constant while speaking. You cannot weave or move your head very much, or your voice will begin to fade in and out. One advantage of a lavaliere microphone (the kind that hangs around your neck) is greater freedom to move about on the platform.

An occasional speaker may look at the microphone rather than at the audience. This can create a comical effect, because it appears to the audience that the speaker is addressing remarks to the microphone rather than to them. If you are a beginning speaker, rehearse in front of a microphone (or makeshift microphone) if at all possible so you can become accustomed to having it in front of you and can learn to speak *into* it but not *at* it.

Also be aware that certain consonant sounds are easily distorted if spoken with too much force into a microphone. Some of the worst offenders are *t, p, b, s, sh, z, g, k,* and *d.* You will want to avoid blasting your listeners or using too much force when uttering these sounds.

Since the presence of a microphone makes certain demands upon a speaker, it is wise to rehearse with a live microphone, particularly before your first microphone speech. If at all possible, secure the room or auditorium in which the microphone will be used for a practice session. Run through your speech several times with the microphone on, and have another person stand or sit at various locations. Even an untrained listener can tell you whether you are coming across clearly or not.

Preparing for Distractions and Interruptions

During the delivery of a speech, unexpected events sometimes occur that cannot be planned for beforehand. Although the list of such potential distractions and interruptions is large, it is a rare speech in which more than one such problem takes place. Speakers, therefore, should not fear that a string of major disasters is likely to occur every time a speech is to be delivered. On the other hand, being aware of the problems that can arise will prepare you to deal with one confidently should it occur.

Some interruptions distract the audience's attention only briefly. Noisy jets may fly over the building. A latecomer may interrupt while finding a seat. You may lose your place or stumble over words. People may cough or shuffle their feet. Whatever the cause, these brief interruptions do little harm to the listeners' basic interest in you and your topic. The best way to handle such noises and distractions is to pause briefly until the room is quiet, then proceed as if nothing had happened. Making a comment about this kind of interruption simply increases the distraction and usually does more harm than good.

Larger interruptions—the kind that create a major breakdown in the audience's concentration on your speech—need to be handled differently from minor distractions. If a group of people arrives late, for instance, and their attempts to find seats distract a good portion of the audience, the speaker should fall silent and remain quiet until the entire group is settled. The speaker may even help people find seats by pointing out empty chairs, thereby shortening the length of the disturbance. Should a loud noise begin and appear likely to continue for a period of time, the speaker should first attempt to be heard over the noise or ask the audience to move closer to the speaker's stand, if possible. If the problem proves impossible to overcome, the speaker may have to abandon the attempt to deliver the speech.

If a heckler begins to yell at you from the audience, handle the situation with dignity and poise. First, remember that the audience came to hear you speak, not the heckler, and their sympathy is basically with you. When this type of disruption first occurs, it is usually best to ignore the heckler and attempt to be heard in between the interruptions. If the heckler's comments are too frequent or too loud to permit the audience to hear you, members of the audience may attempt to quiet the heckler themselves. As the speaker, you should provide sufficient time for this to occur, since a heckler usually loses heart quickly when it becomes obvious that the audience does not support the disturbance. Only when all this has failed should you address the heckler directly, with a calm and dignified comment such as, "Sir (or Madam), I will be happy to try to field any questions or comments from the audience as soon as I have finished my prepared remarks." Under no circumstances should you engage in a shouting match with a heckler, since this gives the intruder precisely what was hoped for—a major share of your audience's attention.

CHAPTER FIVE

Speaking to Inform

$\mathcal{T}$hus far we have talked about elements of public speaking that are more or less generic—how you overcome stage fright, prepare your speech, choose effective language, and verbally and nonverbally deliver a speech are essentially the same, regardless of your topic. There are certain elements of public speaking , however, that do differ according to speech type. These are the topic of the next several chapters.

Recall from Chapter 2 that the majority of speeches are given to inform or persuade an audience. Speeches to inform will be discussed in this chapter, while speeches to persuade will be discussed in Chapter 6.

In Chapter 7, we will consider other types of speeches, such as speeches of introduction, speeches of presentation and acceptance, keynote addresses, and speeches to entertain, among others. Following these discussions is an appendix in which models of several speech types are presented for your review.

When you give a speech to inform, your basic purpose is to provide your listeners with information they do not already have. Even though the audience may have some general knowledge of your topic before you begin, the object of an informative speech is to impart new knowledge or more in-depth information on that topic. Speeches given to inform serve many useful functions in everyday business and professional life. Reports at business meetings, training sessions, client presentations, tours through plants, speeches given at civic clubs—these all are examples of informative speeches. It is important to note that a speech is considered informative whenever the speaker's *primary* purpose is to impart new knowledge, even if the speaker has other motives as well. For example, a new CEO embarking upon changing certain company policies will inevitably need to both explain the changes (informative) and attempt to get subordinates to accept those changes (persuasive).

In this chapter, we will talk about the important elements of an informative speech. For simplicity's sake, the chapter is divided into four parts: the beginning of the speech, the "message" section, the conclusion, and the question-and-answer period.

BEGINNING AN INFORMATIVE SPEECH

Many speech authorities consider the introduction the most important part of any speech because listeners quite often base their opinions about a speech on their first impressions, thus determining how they receive the entire speech. Because of the importance of the introduction, a large portion of this chapter is devoted to ways you can make your introductions effective. There are five imperative factors in a successful introduction: gaining the audience's attention, building interest in the topic, previewing the topic, applying the message to the audience, and establishing your ethos, or credibility, as a speaker.

Gaining the Audience's Attention

The first and perhaps most important way you can use an introduction is to attract the audience's attention. If a speaker fails to gain the audience's attention at the beginning of a speech, it is highly unlikely that the speech will ever fulfill its purpose. Most audience members will mentally "test" a speaker for the first few moments of a speech, giving the speaker their full attention. But if the material sounds dull or uninteresting, their attention will quickly turn to other matters—the agenda for their next meeting, tonight's dinner plans, or just about anything except what the speaker is saying. Therefore, one of the speaker's first tasks is to *demand* the listeners' attention through the use of attention-getting devices. Over centuries of speechmaking, certain types of material have proven effective and become widely accepted for this purpose. These are: humor, stories or anecdotes, common ground, shock, and suspense. Let's look at each attention-getting device in detail.

HUMOR. Nearly everyone enjoys a good joke, so most audiences will automatically pay attention to a speaker who uses humor. Humor that is closely related to one's speech topic, the occasion, or the audience is usually more effective, however, than just a standard joke. This is because a related funny incident serves as a smooth transition into the main body of the speech and retains your audience's attention, whereas when a standard joke ends, so might your audience's interest. Notice how this approach was used at the start of a speech on the safety of commercial airline travel:

> Last week, shortly after the takeoff of a Boeing 727 at Chicago's O'Hare Airport, the passengers heard a voice over the intercom: "Ladies and gentlemen, you are privileged to be the first passengers on an historic flight. There is no pilot or copilot in this aircraft. Your entire flight today from takeoff to landing is being controlled by a system of electronic tapes from the ground. You need not worry in the least. These tapes have been thoroughly tested, and have been found to be completely foolproof . . . foolproof . . . foolproof . . . foolproof . . ."

This lighthearted opening to the speaker's subject gave him a natural opportunity to turn his audience's attention to the more serious issues involved in airline safety.

Some people are more effective at being funny than others. Therefore, before you attempt to use humor in a public speech, ask yourself whether you are an effective humorist. If you are able to make friends laugh in private conversations or at a party, you have probably developed an ability to be humorous. On the other hand, if you seldom get a laugh when you wish to, it is advisable to wait until you have had a chance to develop this technique before using it in a speech introduction. Attempting humor in a public speech and having it fall flat can deflate the speaker's confidence and often does more harm than good. As noted banker and humorist John L. Harlin has noted, "I've seen more than one speaker open a presentation clumsily with a joke just tacked on like an obligatory regulatory filing. When it dies, the audience was lost."

If you are an effective humorist, you must also be cautious: do not give in to the temptation to overuse humor. Treat humor like a spice—a little bit is helpful; too much can destroy the "flavor" of your speech. Audiences respect a speaker who can be both humorous and serious, but if the purpose of the speech is to inform, then listeners expect to be informed, not merely entertained. Use humor sparingly as an attention-getting device.

Finally, make sure any humor you use is in good taste. Do not demean or denigrate any person or group of people in your jokes. John Harlin suggests you ask yourself these questions about any joke you are considering: Is it sexist? Could it be construed as racist or anti-Semitic? Might it be considered off-color? If you think the answer to any of these questions might be yes, don't tell the joke. Although some members of your audience may chuckle at offensive humor, their respect for you will most likely decrease. A speaker's character is one of his or her most potent means of influence with listeners, therefore a joke that is offensive will do nothing but harm you. It will diminish your credibility in the minds of your audience and make it that much harder for you gain their serious attention.

ANECDOTES. A story does not need to be funny in order to be fascinating and to secure the attention of an audience. Anecdotes are short stories that are interesting or biographical in nature (and they can be humorous, as well). Speakers who use anecdotes in their introductions are almost certain to gain their listeners' attention. As with humor, a story that has a natural connection with the speech topic is far better than one without any connection.

Notice the effective way in which this speaker gained audience attention by starting with the following biographical anecdote related to his speech on information technology, then transitioned quickly into previewing his topic:

> Good afternoon. My topic today—information technology— could be a little indigestible coming right after lunch, so I'll make it as palatable for you as I can. Let's ease into it by talking about the technology of another time.
>
> I was born in a small town in Kansas, long enough ago so that any kind of modern technology was pretty rare, and long enough ago that we still had the quaint practice of holding town meetings. I remember one of those meeting at which the main subject was the terrible indignity our town had suffered recently at the hands of a neighboring town. It was even smaller than ours, and clearly less prestigious, but it had stolen a march on us by purchasing a brand-new high-falutin' rheostat-controlled electric chandelier for its town hall. And they were embarrassing us all

over the county by talking up their advanced status and our backwardness.

So the debate that day was about whether or not we should allocate the money—nearly a third of the town's whole budget for the year—to buy our own rheostat-controlled electric chandelier. There were good arguments advanced on both sides of the issue, some thinking that to buy this new electric gadget would be an unnecessary waste of money that could be better spent on fixing the leak in the water tower, others insisting that it was intolerable to continue to exist in the humiliating situation of being thought inferior to those bumpkins down the road.

Finally, the mayor called the question. "Before we vote on this momentous matter," he said, "I would like to know one final thing. Is there anyone in town who actually knows how to play one of these rheostat-controlled chandeliers?"

We have one of those chandelier technologies in this era, too, and by now, most of you have heard the "All Digital, Simultaneous, Real-Time, Interactive, Broadband, Multimedia, Information Superhighway Blues," and you are probably wondering if you can ever learn to play it on your harmonica. I'm going to try to help you in the next few minutes with some facts about just what this new Information Superhighway is, what it offers you as individuals and as civic and business leaders, and, most important, why you should take an active interest in its development.

Avoid the temptation to make the story too detailed or too lengthy—in fact, the story above is about maximum length. Many stories need to be shortened and adapted to a particular speech, especially if the entire speech is rather short. In other words, a five-minute story as an attention-getting device in a ten-minute speech is too long. Keep in mind the general rule that speech introductions should usually account for only about ten percent of the total speech.

COMMON GROUND. The common ground technique is another widely used means of gaining listener attention. When using this device, speakers begin by identifying hobbies, interests, careers, experiences, or preferences that they share in common with their listeners. The common ground technique includes anything that highlights the fact that speaker and listeners share common interests. Examples of common ground are similarities in political or religious background, ethnic heritage, or interest in certain sports. When Richard Lidstad, Vice-President of Human Resources for 3M, delivered a speech honoring students at the University of Minnesota's Carlson

School of Management, he began by establishing common ground with his audience:

> I was asked to talk to you today because I have always felt a strong, personal link to the University of Minnesota. My bachelor of science degree was from the University, more years ago than I'd like to remember. My relationship with the University has been strengthened over the last few years, partly because I have been part of the Executive Mentoring Program for MBA students.

The common ground technique gains listener attention most effectively when the similarities between the speaker and listeners are greatest. If there are few real likenesses between you and your listeners on a given occasion, you would be better off choosing another attention-getting device. Do not try to force weak similarities.

Shock. The shock technique is used to demand quick, almost instantaneous attention from an audience. Shock technique consists of mentioning an unusual, frightening, or hard-to-believe fact, statement, or statistic. It usually is used at the very beginning of a speech. The idea is to blow away any mental "cobwebs" in your listeners' heads and startle them into instant mental alertness. Thom Mayer made excellent use of the shock technique in a speech on "The Population Bomb":

> If I were to tell you that there are 3.6 billion people on earth, with more arriving at the rate of 132 per minute, these figures would probably do nothing more than bore you. If, on the other hand, I were to say, "There's a bomb in this room and it could explode any second!" it is likely that I would have your attention, and you would realize the urgency in what I had said. The cold facts, however, are that the bomb I warned you about and the figures I cited are actually one and the same thing. That bomb is known as the Population Bomb, and it is ticking right now in this room and all over the world.

Not only did Thom Mayer ensure listener attention from the first words of his speech, but the statistics led naturally into the main body of his speech on overpopulation. As with humor and anecdotes, the shock technique works best when it is closely tied to the main message of the speech. Also, speakers using the shock technique must always have evidence to prove the shocking statements they make.

Suspense. Suspense is another useful device for developing rapid listener attention in an introduction. Usually suspense is developed by withholding one's theme or topic from the audience for several moments and by hinting at its importance or uniqueness. A speaker who is building suspense talks "around" the topic for several moments, teasing the audience into trying to guess what the topic will be. Marie Ransley used suspense in the following manner at the beginning of a speech:

> "Warning: the green slime is here." It sounds like a creature out of a grade-B horror movie. But unfortunately it's more real than that. *The New York Times Magazine* warns: ". . . a monster has been loosed among us. In . . . countless incidents around the world, one can almost hear the sloshing of the algae as they grow and expand like the mucid mutations of the late-night horror movies, crawling everywhere and smothering life beneath the slime of cells gone berserk."
>
> Yes, algae is the monster and the immediate victims are the country's lakes.

When used as an attention-getting device in an introduction, suspense must be built quickly. A brief amount of suspense makes an audience curious and expectant, but suspense drawn out beyond several moments rapidly loses its effect. The listeners begin to resent the speaker for not "letting them in" on the speech topic.

Building Interest in the Topic

In addition to gaining the listeners' attention, a speaker should build the audience's interest in the speech topic during the introduction. Some topics are naturally more fascinating to certain audiences than others. A speaker who has analyzed the audience beforehand will know whether she or he must build audience interest in the topic or whether the audience is most likely already interested.

Building interest in one's topic is not the same as gaining attention, but many of the same devices may be used to accomplish it. Recall that humor as an attention-getting device works best if it is easily tied to your topic. Telling a humorous incident unrelated to your topic may gain your listeners' attention, but it does nothing toward building their interest in your topic. On the other hand, a topic-related joke can fulfill both of these important functions at once. The same principle holds true for the anecdote and for common ground, shock, and suspense techniques.

There are other effective methods of building interest in the speech topic, as well. These include asking rhetorical questions, asking real questions, and citing relevant quotations.

RHETORICAL QUESTIONS. One common method of building your audience's interest in your topic is to start the speech with rhetorical questions related to the topic. As was explained in Chapter 2, when you ask rhetorical questions, you do not expect an "out-loud" answer from your listeners. Rather, you intend that your listeners will mentally try to answer the questions, thereby generating attention and building interest in the speech topic. Sheila Wellington, president of Catalyst, used rhetorical questions to begin an awards dinner speech:

> Nineteen hundred and ninety-five begins the last half of the last decade of the 20th century. It is a time of extraordinary challenge and change for American society. What do these challenges, these changes mean for women? Will progress be halted? Will the benefits we have brought to the nation's economy be lost?
>
> The answer is clear from the merest backward glance. It is appropriate that on this—Catalyst's 20th annual awards dinner—we take that glance.

Rhetorical questions also serve the purpose of directly challenging your audience. When you ask rhetorical questions that challenge your audience to formulate answers, you generate interest in your own answers as well. You build interest by directing a real challenge to your listeners—by including them.

REAL QUESTIONS. Occasionally, speakers will ask real (as opposed to rhetorical) questions, which they expect audience members to answer aloud. This can be done by a show of hands or by inviting specific listeners to answer aloud. This technique can build topic interest as well as arouse attention, but it is a bit risky. Since the speaker may not receive the expected answer, he or she may be caught off guard and become confused. If you plan to use real questions, prepare to react to various kinds of responses.

QUOTATIONS. Another interest-building technique consists of beginning a speech with a quotation that highlights an important aspect of your topic. The quotation identifies the general topic area for the listeners, provokes thought, and creates a mild suspense about how the speaker will develop the particular topic within a broad area. Audiences are usually interested in the thoughts of others, particularly if quoted from some well-known or well-respected person. Here are two examples:

> Good afternoon. It is a pleasure to be with you. Since the topic of today's meeting is *managing* diversity, I'm reminded of a comment once made by a truly great manager, Casey Stengel, when he was in his prime as manager of the Yankees. One day he was asked about the art of managing.
>
> "Managing," Casey replied, "is getting paid for home runs someone else hits."

We're here today to discuss diversity. It's a difficult issue—an area where it's not always easy to hit home runs.

Thank you for inviting me to spend some time with you this evening. As requested, I'd like to share some thoughts with you on "Successful Strategies for Achieving Your Career Goals."

Someone once asked James Lofton, wide receiver for the Buffalo Bills, what tricks he used to achieve success. Lofton replied, "One trick is to work harder than the other guy. The second trick, always hustle. Third trick, study and know what you're doing. Fourth trick, always be prepared. Fifth, never give up. Those are my tricks."

What Lofton was really saying is that there are no "tricks" for getting ahead, but there are some very basic fundamentals of hard work and planning that can give each of us a competitive edge, if we use them.

Previewing the Topic

On the covers of many paperback books you will find intriguing hints about the contents of the book. These are meant to help sell the book. A speech introduction serves a similar function prior to the main body of the speech. Audiences have learned to expect the speaker to "clue them in" on the speech topic, its purpose, and often the main points that will be covered. Thus, previewing the topic is a significant function of most speech introductions.

The most obvious and straightforward method of previewing the topic consists of simply stating your speech purpose to the audience during the introduction. Sometimes, however, this type of introduction may fail to fulfill the other important functions of an introduction at the same time. An introduction that merely previews the topic, without simultaneously generating attention and building interest in the topic, might be labeled a clear but dull introduction. Notice how this introduction to a speech on modern dental laboratories begins by focusing the listeners' attention, builds their interest in the speaker's subject, and finishes by previewing the topic for the audience:

If you are like me, you hate going to the dentist. Even the remote chance that he or she might find a cavity, followed in rapid-fire order by the pain of the Novocain needle, the siren-like whine of the dreaded drill, and later by the leathery lip which won't allow you to eat with dignity—all this sends shudders through most of us. If you have ever done really serious time in the dentist's chair, say for a root canal or to have a full crown fitted, you probably look upon dental science as a science barely emerging from the Neanderthal Period. Even some of the tools the dentist waves before your eyes remind you of prehistoric instruments, looking about as subtle as stone-headed axes as they are forced inside your gaping mouth.

The truth is, though, that dentistry is a very modern, high-tech science in which measurements must be made in tens of thousandths of a millimeter. Every day, researchers and technicians in dental labs deal in minute expansions and contractions of plasters, wax, gold, and plastic to assure that dental patients will enjoy perfectly fitting dental products. Today I want to share with you some of the fascinating "high-tech" insights I gained, first while working in a dental laboratory and more recently as a practicing dentist.

Again, as you can see, previewing the topic is a very important function of the introduction in speeches given to inform. Because the principal purpose of the speech is to teach, the speaker must make sure the message is received. To ensure audience understanding, good public speakers use several opportunities to restate their message. Previewing the topic in the introduction is the first opportunity to give the listener the basic message in a brief form. If the members of the audience hear the topic previewed in the introduction, are told the complete message in the body of the speech, and then hear the message summarized in the conclusion, most of them are likely to receive the message.

Applying the Message to the Audience

A fourth function of the introduction is a natural follow-up to previewing the topic. As soon as you tell your listeners what you propose to talk about, show them how that topic applies to them—what they stand to gain from hearing the message, why the topic should be of particular interest to them, and why it has significance for them.

Louis Housman applied his message in a speech on "Older Americans" by showing that the speech dealt with a significant topic and by implying that his listeners stood to gain from hearing about this topic:

There are 31 million Americans sixty years and older. They constitute the single largest minority in the nation. This minority, since 1900, is growing at twice the rate of our total population. The way in which these older Americans are viewed by society as a whole, by younger persons, and by themselves, has important implications for all of you concerned with the well-being of older persons.

In short, bring your message home to your listeners by linking it to their interests, needs, and concerns.

Establishing Your *Ethos*

The ancient Greek rhetorician, Aristotle, claimed that three forces influenced an audience: the speaker's logic, appeals to the listeners' emotions, and the character of the speaker. He wrote that the speaker's character, which he called *ethos,* was the most powerful of the three. Although Aristotle was writing about persuasive speaking, and though some modern speech authorities disagree with his ranking of the three elements, no one would claim that the speaker's character and credibility are unimportant, even in informative speeches. We will address this topic more fully in Chapter 6, but it is important to bring it up here as it relates to beginning an informative speech or presentation.

You have undoubtedly noticed how you accept what some people tell you much more readily than you accept the words of others. Since listeners more readily accept information from a source they believe and have confidence in, establishing one's ethos is an important task for a public speaker to accomplish during the introduction of an informative speech. Ethos can be loosely translated into the old salespersons' adage, "You have to sell yourself first." Ethos exists in the minds of the listeners as their inward answers to three unspoken questions:

1. Is this speaker thoroughly familiar with the subject?

2. Is this speaker being completely open and honest with me?

3. Do I enjoy listening to this speaker?

Of course, not all speakers need to begin by establishing their expertise and sincerity. Well-known personalities or speakers fortunate enough to be introduced to their audience by someone else are usually wiser to accept their reputation in modest silence. Other speakers, however, must themselves fulfill the job of convincing the audience of their knowledge, sincerity, and likability. When this job is left up to you, the speaker, you should establish your ethos early, preferably during the introduction. Many of the techniques useful in gaining audience attention and building interest in the speech topic may also aid in building speaker ethos. Humor, for instance, usually increases an audience's enjoyment when listening to a speaker. Devices such as anecdotes and the shock technique can show listeners the speaker has done research and is informed about the topic.

In addition, several specific techniques for building ethos can be used on occasions when you feel a special need to "sell your credentials" to your audience. One of these is straightforwardly mentioning some of the research and preparation you did for the speech. This can be worded into your introduction, not in a bragging way, but simply to show the listeners you have earned the right to speak to them. Here's an example:

> Thank you. You know when I first started out in the publishing business thirty-two years ago, I quickly discovered how much I loved helping authors express themselves. I have spent my career striving to do just that. Today, I'd like to share a bit of what I've learned in the hopes that those of you who share my enthusiasm will carry the torch.

A similar technique of ethos-building consists of mentioning some experience you have had that qualifies you as an "expert" on your topic. Here is an example of such an ethos-builder, related in a speech by John B. Donovan, president of Donovan Public Affairs, to the Westchester County Chamber of Commerce. Part of his speech noted the low odds that someone like him would ever find himself interviewed on national television. Then he said:

> The next year, however, was an election year and I had the chance to write a book about one of the candidates. Before you know it I was on television and radio in twenty-five cities.

In the process of relating his topic to his audience, Donovan also qualified himself as an expert due to his sudden and extensive appearances in the media. Suddenly the speaker becomes "someone who has been there," someone who has earned the right to speak with authority on the topic.

On occasions when you are introduced to the audience prior to your speech, you ordinarily will not want to attempt much, if any, ethos-building of your own. Usually a simple statement such as, "Thank you, Bob," or "Thank you for that kind introduction," is all that is needed. If the introducer has been extremely flattering, you may want to insert a humorous comment to show modesty, as in, "My generous introducer got so carried away, I found myself sitting here trying to imagine who was about to give this marvelous speech!" If, on the other hand, your introducer fails to give you enough credit, you should modestly supply some of the missing facts yourself during the speech introduction. This should be done matter-of-factly, as an attempt to fill in some information the introducer overlooked but which may be important for your audience to know. For example:

> Thank you, Sharon, for that introduction. Something Sharon did not mention was my two years as a Little League umpire. I bring this up because that experience gave birth to many of the ideas about fair play in business, which I will be exploring in my speech tonight.

Imparting the Message of an Informative Speech

The central part of an informative speech, sandwiched between the introduction and conclusion, is called the "body" of the speech. The body contains the essential message of the speech, fully developed. Although each speech is unique, both to the individual speaker and to the speech occasion, and the speech outline plots the speaker's approach to the topic (see Chapter 2), certain general rules must be followed while imparting the message if the informative speech is to have maximum impact. To present an effective message during the body of a speech, the speaker must maintain the audience's attention, react to audience feedback, make smooth transitions, avoid becoming too technical, and personalize the speech.

Maintaining the Audience's Attention

Gaining the audience's attention at the start of a speech or presentation does not guarantee the speaker unbroken attention for the rest of the speech. Since people's attention usually focuses on one person or idea only briefly and shifts constantly from one object to another, a public speaker must make a constant effort to keep the listeners focused on the message.

Most of the attention-getting devices that are useful during the introduction of an informative speech may also be sprinkled throughout the speech to maintain listener attention. A joke or anecdote, a set of shocking statistics, or a bit of suspense during the body of the speech can regain flagging attention and renew audience interest.

Careful preparation regarding nonverbal attention factors can also help to effectively capture and retain audience attention. The way your audience is seated, for instance, is one of these nonverbal attention factors. Speakers have found that the closer the audience members are to one another, the higher their attention generally remains. This seems to be because audience members generate attention among themselves, thus relieving the speaker of part of the task of keeping their attention. Therefore, whenever you find yourself facing a sparse or scattered audience, with numerous empty chairs among your listeners, invite the audience to sit more closely together in front rows. Maintaining their attention throughout your speech will prove considerably easier.

A second nonverbal attention factor relates to listening conditions. The more you, the speaker, can ensure comfortable conditions for effective listening, the more likely you will be to have the continuous attention of your audience. Whenever possible, arrive at the speaking location before your audience to arrange for proper listening conditions.

Reacting to Audience Feedback

As you proceed through your speech, be alert to audience reactions and respond to them whenever necessary. Reacting to audience feedback is not a technique a beginning speaker can typically acquire all at once during a first or second speech. It is an important skill to develop, however, since a public speech involves two-way communication just as a conversation does. Not to show any reaction to audience feedback may cause some listeners to feel you are ignoring them. Indeed, many audiences may find this lack of response insulting.

In order to respond to feedback, you must first learn to interpret it. As you begin giving speeches you will notice that some listeners react more vigorously than others do. Some people will appear more interested, more alert, and more intense in their reactions. Pay closer attention to these individuals as you speak and look for signs of understanding, puzzlement, agreement, or disagreement in their faces, in their posture, and in their eyes. Once you have developed the ability to recognize positive and negative reactions, you can begin to adjust your message, language, and delivery techniques a bit to lessen negative reactions and increase positive forms of feedback.

Adjust especially to audience reaction if it comes from a sizable proportion of your listeners. If only one or two listeners frown, for instance, their actions may only mean that they did not understand or did not agree with something you just said. However, if 30 or 40 percent of your listeners frown, whatever you just said probably needs repeating or clarifying.

Making Smooth Transitions

A transition is like a switch on a railroad line. It allows a speaker to change from one aspect of the topic to another. Well-planned transitions go unnoticed by the listeners but give them an impression of a smoothly flowing speech. Conversely, not planning one's transitions results in jerky shifts from one main point to another, making the speech sound like a series of disconnected mini-speeches.

A transition accomplishes three purposes: first, it summarizes the point you have just finished; second, it tells your listeners what you will cover next; finally, it shows the relationship between the two. Usually a good transition does all of this as briefly as possible. Transitions between major points (the main headings on your outline) may consist of a sentence or two that relates what you have just finished saying to what you will say next. For instance, if you were giving a speech in which you were relating how you got your first job and were moving from your early rejections to the company that finally hired you, your transition might sound something like this:

> After those fourteen rejection letters had thoroughly shattered my hopes of ever getting a position came the happy day when the fifteenth company's interviewer called me and announced, "We'd like you to come and work with us."

Speakers also commonly plan major transitions by selecting a key word or phrase to make one point and then using it again to make the next point. Notice in this classic example how President John F. Kennedy linked the past to the present by focusing on the past and present tenses of the verb *summons* in this transition in his inaugural address:

> Since this country was founded, each generation of Americans has been summoned to give testimony to its national loyalty. The graves of young Americans who answered the call to service surround the globe.
>
> Now the trumpet summons us again—not as a call to bear arms, though arms we need—not as a call to battle, though embattled we are—but a call to bear the burden of a long twilight struggle, year in and year out, "rejoicing in hope, patient in tribulation"—a struggle against the common enemies of man: tyranny, poverty, disease and war itself.

Transitions between minor points (subheads) can often be made with just a word or phrase, such as "First," "Second," "On the other hand," "Therefore," or "Moreover," as in the following short example (italics added):

> Communications professionals can take three steps in order to help effectively manage the alliance process. *First,* get on the radar screen. *Once there,* get selected for the team. *Finally,* contribute on a level where everybody recognizes the real value, in terms of shareholder value, that your process is bringing.

Regardless of the type, transitions must be thoroughly planned and rehearsed, not left to chance. Word-for-word memorization may be useful when rehearsing transitions to ensure they will tie the parts of the speech together clearly.

Avoiding Becoming Too Technical

Imagine you are listening to a speech in which an expert in Total Quality Management (TQM) is explaining how his or her organization first launched a TQM program. You hear the speaker say:

> So at that time I took a good amount of schooling on statistical methods and process, the Taguchi-designed experiments, Deming seminars, as well as Juran. We decided it was time we turned

from analysis inspection to prevention, what we call a "detection-to-prevention" mode of operation. We use a term called CPK, which stands for capability of the process' indices. Based on the CPK of our processes, I know within statistical variations what the analysis will be of a product we're going to ship out of the plant.

Chances are, unless you are also an expert in TQM, you wouldn't pay attention to the speech for very long. Even if you tried to pay attention, you might wind up with a severe headache within five minutes! What is wrong with such a speech? The speaker is using too much technical language. The information is quite accurate, but it is expressed in language generally understood only by people trained in TQM. To get the point across to novices, the speaker must first translate the ideas into more common words—language that a lay person readily understands but does not find condescending. For instance, the TQM speaker might simply have said, "After learning quite a bit about TQM, we devised a way to ensure the quality level of every product we ship out of our plant."

You can make almost any topic understandable to any audience to a certain degree, but highly technical topics demand first that you be an expert in the area, then that you take great pains in simplifying your language to ensure audience understanding. Finally, technical topics delivered to a nontechnical audience should not be telescoped into a five- or ten-minute speech. Complex ideas, even when put into common language, require sufficient time for the speaker to define and explain and for the listeners to absorb fully.

Personalizing Your Speech

Probably nothing maintains the attention and interest of an audience as well as including a number of stories, examples, and humor involving people because, to put it simply, people are interested in people. The speaker who frequently brings people into his or her speeches is personalizing the speech and making it more interesting.

Suppose you are speaking about the effects of radiation—the kind of radiation emitted by such ordinary items as video display terminals. You could give your listeners tons of statistics showing how many people are affected by such radiation each year, and how many additional health-care dollars it takes to treat them. *Some* statistics of that sort would be very helpful. But if you want to be certain of regaining your listeners' wavering attention following a string of numbers, give them an example with a person in it, such as the following:

> Becky Krimson worked for the Citizens National Bank. Throughout her three-year period of employment there, Becky often complained of headaches, dizziness, fatigue, and loss of hair. Her boss

said she occasionally suffered partial memory loss, while her co-workers frequently complained about Becky's emotional instability. Upon a visit to her doctor she was given some pills, told to take a few days' rest, and sent home. At the time, Becky did not know that the video display terminal she worked with at the bank was zapping her with radiation and that rest and pills could not cure her symptoms.

Personalizing your speech does not mean you must always use real people as examples. You might create a fictional person who is meant to stand for the "average" individual in certain circumstances. In so doing, you are able to present your information in story form rather than as a string of statistics. One speaker created Vladimir, a typical Russian importer, for a speech on business practices in the Confederation of Independent States. By tracing Vladimir's dealings with his customers, the speaker was able to show her listeners how Russian business practices are similar to and different from those in the United States.

CONCLUDING AN INFORMATIVE SPEECH

Speech conclusions are typically brief, accounting for only about five percent of the total speech. However, the conclusion may represent the most important part of many speeches because the audience hears the conclusion last and is therefore likely to remember it the longest. You should use as much care in preparing your conclusion as you did your introduction. As in introductions, there are several key elements to successful speech conclusions. Audiences typically expect speakers to summarize the speech's main ideas, reinforce the central idea, and psychologically close the speech. Before listeners are able to pick out these guideposts, however, they must know when the conclusion of the speech begins. Therefore, your first job in concluding a speech is to give your audience a clear signal that you are about to conclude.

Signaling Your Conclusion

How do you send this signal? One of the simplest ways is by beginning your conclusion with phrases such as "In closing," "I want to conclude today by saying," or "Here's the message I'd like you to leave with today." A second, more subtle way is through changes in your wording and your manner of delivery. By an extra long pause prior to your conclusion, by changes in vocal tone, volume, and pacing, or by moving a few steps as you start your conclusion, you can signal the end of your speech. Your wording, too, becomes "larger," more grand in tone as you return to the general theme with which you began the speech. In this way, without actually saying "in conclusion," you clearly signal your audience that you are about to close. Notice how effectively Kathy Weisensel concluded her speech dealing with misconceptions about the victims of mental retardation:

> While misconceptions are slow to pass away, they must surely die. Our nation's retarded are not mentally ill, totally ineducable, or incapable of happy and productive lives.
>
> I know, in a deeply personal way, the pain that these misconceptions inspire. But I also know that the world is changing. I have a deep faith that you and others of our generation will reject the senseless and destructive stereotypes of the past. As Bernard Posner has said: "The young people of the world seem to be forging a new set of values. It appears to be a value system of recognizing the intrinsic worth of all humans, retarded or not, . . . a value system of acceptance: of accepting life as it is, and people as they are."
>
> Thank you for your acceptance.

Summarizing the Main Ideas

The summary is the main part of a speech conclusion. Although a conclusion may have other functions as well, its principal function is summarizing the major ideas, especially in an informative speech. This is generally accomplished through restatement—repeating the same ideas but in different words. Observe how one speaker summarized an informative speech on changing health-care patterns:

> It is time to decentralize the health system once again, to shift the responsibility for health back to the workplace and the home and from there to the individual and his or her family. In short, it is time to revolutionize health care in America. Only by doing so will we enable all people, no matter who they are or where they live, to manage their own lives more effectively and more healthfully.

In this speaker's summary, the main ideas of the entire speech were again presented in brief form. Even without reading the entire speech, you were able to know the topic of the speech and its main points.

Reinforcing the Central Idea

Because your conclusion is your last chance to impress the central message of your speech upon your listeners, you will often try to do this in several ways. A summary, of course, typically restates the central idea, but often simply restating it fails to "brand" it into the listeners' minds. Additional means of reinforcing the central idea include ending the speech with a quotation, concluding with a dramatic statement of your own, and referring back to the introduction.

ENDING WITH A QUOTATION. Concluding your speech with a quotation is usually a successful way of ensuring that the audience will remember your speech. Here is how Rosetta M. Riley concluded a speech on Cadillac's commitment to quality:

> We recognize that we're not where we need to be with respect to quality. Cadillac has a long heritage of process quality leadership. Our founder, Henry Leland, led his engineers by the motto "Craftsmen, a creed; accuracy, a law." In the last six years we have recalled that motto frequently. We share Leland's commitment and we continue to strive to make every Cadillac a great Cadillac.

Like Riley's, closing quotations are especially effective when they relate closely to the central message of the speech and are brief.

DRAMATIC STATEMENT OF YOUR OWN. A dramatic statement that you make up is another way of impressing your basic message upon the listeners as you conclude. In this example, the speaker impassionately asks businesses to care about the welfare of humankind:

> In the last analysis, the very concept of individual freedom is at stake! It is hard for most Americans to realize that the survival of the very idea for which this nation stands is not inevitable. It will survive *only* if enough Americans care enough.

While most conclusions cannot be so sensational, many can be riveting enough to cause the listeners to remember your closing words longer than when the ending is simply matter-of-fact.

A twist of surprise and some well-planned wording can sometimes make all the difference, too. The same speaker concluded his speech by recalling the notion of the three R's many of us remember from grammar school to create a climactic ending to his speech and simultaneously summarize his main points: "Reason, Realism, and Relevance—perhaps we might think of these as the three R's in our search for the most appropriate involvement." In all likelihood, listeners left the speech remembering at least those words.

REFERENCE BACK TO INTRODUCTION. A third method by which to reinforce your speech's central idea in the conclusion is by referring back to your introduction. Since the introduction nearly always contains a preview of the speech's purpose, a reference back to it in the conclusion serves to implant that purpose firmly in the listeners' minds. A speaker who opened her speech by stating that "Disney World in Florida is really not a Mickey Mouse organization; it is truly big business!" concluded her speech in the following way:

> I hope I have given you a sense of the scope and complexity involved in running the Magic Kingdom. Were you allowed to see behind the scenes—behind the fairyland to the maze of computers, behind Donald Duck and Goofy to the army of interviewers screening job applicants, behind Cinderella's Castle and the Monorail to the planners and risk takers who constantly pour millions of dollars into this fantasy world—you would recognize that Disney World is by no means a Mickey Mouse operation. It is truly big business!

Closing the Speech Psychologically

Audiences not only want to *know* a speech is over; they want to *feel* that it is complete, too. Did you ever have to leave an exciting basketball game shortly before it ended? You were probably left with a feeling of incompleteness that was not erased by later reading the final score in the newspaper. Similarly, speech audiences expect speakers to tidy up any loose ends during their conclusions. In addition to restating the main points and refocusing on the central idea, speakers frequently should finish by involving their listeners in the topic one more time. There are several means of doing this, including challenging the audience, asking rhetorical questions, and repeating an already stated theme or slogan.

CHALLENGING THE AUDIENCE. Lee Iacocca recalls issuing challenges to his audiences in numerous speeches: "I threw my arguments right into the front row and asked the audience what they were willing to do to help solve the problems I was talking about. There has to be call to action. You can't let your audience off the hook. They have to leave the auditorium wanting to do something."

Here's an example of such a challenge:

> The time has come for us to light that fire! Our children need your help to light the fire under America. Won't you please join with us to save the dream for the children of America? Thank you.

RHETORICAL QUESTIONS. Rhetorical questions can involve the audience at least as effectively when used in your conclusion as in the introduction.

When used at the end of a speech, they often linger in the listener's mind because no answer was provided. They can cause individual listeners to keep trying to provide satisfactory answers for themselves well after the speech has ended. For instance, if you are a person who is always late, would you later rethink this speaker's closing rhetorical question?

> So remember, people who are always late aren't just disorganized. There are three possible reasons for repeated lateness: first, they could be trying to defy authority; second, they could be trying to gain power over the other person; and, finally, they could be trying to live up to stereotypes about groups of people. Could any of these reasons describe you?

REPETITION OF A THEME OR SLOGAN. A final method of psychologically closing a speech is by repeating a theme or slogan first mentioned in the introduction. This technique is similar to referring back to your central purpose, except here you are trying to plant a brief statement in the listener's memory—a theme or slogan that will vividly recall your speech to mind. Preachers sometimes use this approach when they begin a sermon with a Bible verse, then close by repeating it word-for-word.

As a final word on conclusions, remember that whichever techniques you use to close your speeches, every informative speech needs some form of conclusion. Never end with your last main point. The audience expects you to "put it all together" before you sit down. Conclusions need not be lengthy—as a matter of fact, they should almost always be brief—but they must always be there!

CONDUCTING A QUESTION-AND-ANSWER PERIOD

Informative speeches or presentations are frequently followed by a question-and-answer period. It is not uncommon for audience members to learn as much or sometimes even more detail about the speaker's topic in the question-and-answer period. This is because a listener with a specific question will usually remember the speaker's answer longer than everything else that was said.

Question-and-answer periods are also helpful for you, the speaker, in several ways. First, they provide you with an opportunity to learn to think on your feet by forcing you to extemporize when responding to a specific question. Once you become expert in responding to questions from the floor, your answers actually provide for a more dynamic interaction with your audience. This makes question-and-answer periods more informative and often more enjoyable for the listeners.

The two key points of discussion here are how to invite questions from your audience and how to answer them.

Inviting Questions

You will generally know whether or not a question-and-answer period is likely to follow a speech. In a client presentation, for example, you can rest assured that questions will certainly follow. Additionally, some clubs and organizations consider such a session traditional. Or you may anticipate your topic arousing enough interest to cause a number of audience members to ask questions. Regardless of the situation, whenever you expect a question-and-answer period to follow a speech it is a good idea to invite such a session when you begin your speech. Mentioning at the start that you will be happy to respond to any questions when you have finished gives the listeners a chance to develop questions during your talk. When a speaker ends the speech with "Now, are there any questions?" without giving any prior warning, the audience is caught off guard and often cannot form any significant questions quickly.

Once a question-and-answer session has begun, the speaker must be as impartial as possible in recognizing listeners who have questions. Naturally, preference should be given to the first hands raised over the later ones and to those who have not yet asked a question over those who have already had a turn. If there is a prearranged time limit for questions, or if you feel that the audience is getting bored or that your questions are becoming repetitive, you can provide a warning that you are about to close the session. For example, you might make a comment such as, "I believe we have time for only two more questions. I'll recognize the woman in the second row, then the man in the rear."

Answering Questions

If you are thoroughly prepared and knowledgeable about your speech topic, you will be able to answer most questions easily. Occasionally, of course, a question will be raised to which you do not know the answer. When this occurs, simply respond, "I'm sorry, I can't answer that question." When you give such a response in an informative speech, you will not appear to be avoiding the question but merely indicating a lack of knowledge on your part. Audiences do not expect speakers to be all-knowing on any topic, so the occasional use of this response causes no one embarrassment.

If you have used one or more visual aids during an informative speech and someone asks a question related to a particular visual, be certain you bring it back into full view of the audience before responding to the question. This allows listeners to perceive your answer through two channels, verbal and visual. You may also wish to point to a particular part of a visual while responding, if the question relates specifically to that part.

When you are asked a question requiring both a direct answer plus some explanation, provide the direct answer first, then the explanation. Usually the questioner is more interested in the factual answer than in a list of reasons or causes, and making the person wait for the core of the answer can irk the questioner. Occasionally, you may feel there is strong justification for reversing this order, but ordinarily give the direct answer first followed by the explanation.

Finally, be complete and concise in answering questions. Avoid, on the one hand, single-word answers such as Yes or No. On the other hand, once you have answered the question, stop. Do not be tempted to ramble on with fascinating information that strays too far from the topic and may only serve to bore your listeners. If the matter is fairly technical in nature and requires some explanation for a complete answer, by all means give the explanation, then stop. Often there may be several others in your audience anxiously waiting to ask a question that is very special to them.

CHAPTER SIX

*S*peaking to Motivate and Persuade

*W*hile speeches to inform are the most common type of speech, a second and no less important purpose of many speeches is to persuade. A speech given to persuade has as its principle goal the influencing of the attitudes, beliefs, or behavior of the listeners. All of us have numerous opportunities for persuasive speaking, either professionally or personally. Professionally, salespeople try to make sales with persuasive speaking. Lawyers use persuasion to secure a jury's decision. Stock brokers speak persuasively for or against the purchase of a certain investment. On a more personal level, you might want to convince members of your PTA to take a certain stand on the school budget, tell your city council why you believe they should vote for an ordinance you favor, or explain to other members of a volunteer organization why a certain fundraising method should be employed. All would be exercises in persuasion.

Each of the general principles of public speaking discussed in earlier chapters applies to persuasive speaking. Persuasive speaking, however, is more difficult than speaking to inform and thus demands additional skills, which we will discuss in this chapter. Remember Aristotle's three primary sources of persuasion, which we addressed briefly in Chapter 5? These, along with responsibility, are the additional skills a persuasive speaker must possess. Before we address them, however, we will begin with discussions about the definition and types of persuasive speeches.

UNDERSTANDING TYPES OF PERSUASIVE SPEECHES

Persuasive speeches are given in situations in which two or more points of view about a topic are in conflict. The persuasive speaker tries to convince those who disagree that his or her point of view is the correct one. Put another way, persuasive speeches are given when there is some question about which view is correct. Three types of questions give rise to persuasive speech situations: questions of fact, questions of value, and questions of policy.

Understanding Questions of Fact

Questions of fact deal with occurrences and the reasons that they have happened, are happening, or will happen in the future. Here are several examples of purpose sentences for persuasive speeches dealing with questions of fact:

- My purpose is to persuade my audience that a major earthquake will hit California within the next five years.
- My purpose is to convince my audience that the Ebola virus is one of the most deadly viruses to come along in years.
- My purpose is to persuade my audience that side-impact airbags will save thousands of lives over a ten-year period.

Notice that each speech purpose deals with occurrences about which there is some element of doubt. If it were now a solidly proven fact that side-impact airbags did indeed save thousands of lives over a ten-year period, there would be no reason for anyone to give a persuasive speech on the subject; we would all know it to be true. The same can be said of topics that relate to the present, such as airport security and political terrorism, and, of course, to those dealing with the future, such as a California earthquake, since nothing in the future can yet be considered an established fact.

Understanding Questions of Value

Are certain kinds of DNA research morally justifiable? What are the ethical responsibilities of journalists? These are questions of value. Although such questions involve matters of fact, they go further. They also call for judgments about right and wrong, ethical and unethical, good and bad, proper and improper. "How many journalists are there in Washington, D.C.?" is purely a question of fact because it involves statistics. However, a question such as, "What are the ethical responsibilities of journalists when writing a story about improving care for the elderly?" goes much further; it demands a moral judgment. A person's answer to this second question depends not only on his or her knowledge about medical care for the elderly but also on his or her moral values. Notice how the following purpose sentences for speeches of value also require this kind of judgment:

- My purpose is to persuade my listeners that the state should have a better food-stamp program.
- My purpose is to persuade my audience that in the long run it still pays to buy American-made cars.
- My purpose is to persuade my clients that our company will provide better service than our competitors.

Understanding Questions of Policy

Questions about policy deal with whether certain courses of action should be taken. They include matters of both fact and value within themselves but go beyond them to consider what should or should not be done. A question such as, "What steps should be taken to control the problem of car theft?" demands both that the audience know certain facts about car theft and that they consider it wrong. Once this is established, the speaker can go further to advocate that one or more solutions be carried out. Here are some examples of purpose sentences for speeches dealing with questions of policy. Notice that most policy-related purpose sentences contain the word *should:*

- My purpose is to show my audience that a permanent site should be established for the Olympic Games.

- My purpose is to persuade my listeners that stricter controls should be placed on our division's travel policies.

- My purpose is to convince my audience that achieving adequate employment should be our number one priority.

Considering Three Sources of Persuasion

Before people will believe, think, or do something, they must *want* to do it. Persuasion is simply a means by which one person can cause another to *want* to believe, think, or do. We all adopt new beliefs, attitudes, and actions constantly. Think for a moment about why you might decide to see a certain film, admire a certain singer, or choose a particular product in the grocery store. Basically, each decision is made only when you want to make it. Whenever someone else tries to convince you to decide a certain way, that person is using the process of persuasion.

Over 2,500 years ago, Aristotle wrote a book on persuasion called *Rhetoric,* which is still considered by nearly all speech scholars to be the most influential book written on the subject. In it, Aristotle stated that there are three primary sources by which people can be persuaded: *pathos,* which means the listeners' own personal drives, needs, and desires; *ethos,* which is the way in which an audience perceives the character and personality of the speaker; and *logos,* meaning the listeners' own thinking processes. Persuaders must concentrate on each of these factors. They must know their listeners' needs, establish their own prestige, and build logical arguments that their listeners can follow. A knowledgeable, sincere, logical speaker stands a good chance of successfully persuading others. Let's look at each of these three persuasive forces in detail.

Pathos: Analyzing the Needs of Your Listeners

Most people like to consider themselves very logical creatures. They prefer to think they make decisions and behave in certain ways based solely on logic. But if they were to make an honest analysis of the reasons for much of their behavior and many of their decisions, they would probably be forced to admit that they are sometimes not logical at all. Unlike Lieutenant Data of *Star Trek: The Next Generation,* people frequently believe, decide, or act in particular ways simply because they want to or need to, rather than because reason or logic points to their choices.

Therefore, if you plan to persuade people you must appeal not only to their brains, but to their needs and desires—their *pathos*—as well. Is such an appeal beneath the dignity of a persuader? No, so long as the needs and desires to which you appeal are legitimate, and you honestly believe in the cause you are promoting.

Discovering the Basic Needs of Your Audience

As we discussed in Chapter 2, all good speakers must analyze their audiences' knowledge and interest levels prior to organizing the speech. The effective persuader must go one step further: he or she must also seek out the special needs and attitudes of the audience in order to plan the persuasion strategy most suited to that group of listeners. Indeed, in a persuasive speech the success or failure of your presentation can largely depend on how well you know your audience beforehand.

Audiences may have hundreds of special needs and attitudes, depending on the subject of a given speech and the listeners' previous experiences with the topic. As they pertain to organizing your speech, these myriad needs and attitudes can be grouped according to how they affect the audiences' reception of you and your topic. Essentially, audiences fall into four basic categories on a scale between "very positive" and "very negative": the positive audience, the neutral audience, the disinterested audience, and the opposed audience. Each has a different set of needs and must be approached differently by the speaker. You will want to determine your audiences' prespeech attitudes as carefully as possible on this scale so you can prepare the best approach.

POSITIVE AUDIENCE. The positive audience is one that already agrees with your basic persuasive purpose. If you are speaking to librarians about the need to raise money for the local library, for instance, most of your listeners are likely to be in favor of your idea before you begin. Similarly, if you are speaking to co-workers about the need to oppose a rumored salary freeze, most of your audience will be likely to support your idea. Of course, this is the easiest type of audience to persuade. Your only persuasive task with a positive audience is to deepen their feelings about the topic. Their basic need is simply for a "recharging."

NEUTRAL AUDIENCE. The neutral audience has a different need. They are neither for nor against your topic—they simply do not know very much about it. Therefore, their basic need is for information that will make it possible for them to form an opinion. Suppose you are trying to sell a new dishwashing detergent, and the people in your audience have never heard of it before. If you are going to persuade them to buy it, you must first give them some information about it. You might, for example, tell them that it washes more dishes per bottle than brand X, smells better than brand Y, cleans better than brand Z, and is easier on the hands than all three! In so doing, you are helping them determine that your brand is the brand to buy.

DISINTERESTED AUDIENCE. The disinterested audience knows about the topic but couldn't care less. They consider it a dull issue or an unimportant one, not particularly relevant to them or their needs. This kind of audience needs to be "electrified." They need to be shown the seriousness of the problem, the closeness of the danger, or the way in which they will be affected. In short, before they can be persuaded to do anything, they must be motivated to care.

OPPOSED AUDIENCE. The last group is the opposed audience—the most difficult kind of audience for a persuasive speaker to face. It is composed of people who disagree with your stand on the topic. They feel as strongly about the issues as you do, but they have opposing opinions. Sometimes they may distrust you simply because you hold a viewpoint different from theirs. Their need is first for open-mindedness, then for conviction. You must first succeed in getting a fair hearing for your side, then attempt to convince them of your viewpoint.

How do you discover whether you will be facing a positive, neutral, disinterested, or opposed audience? Usually by the same methods mentioned in the "Analyzing Your Audience" section of Chapter 2. Ask the person who invites you to speak about the attitudes and needs of your prospective listeners. Ask friends and acquaintances who know your future audience members. Talk to other speakers who have addressed the same group in the past. In each case, ask questions designed to tell you about their needs in relationship to the topic. If, for example, you are planning a speech that strongly advocates greater freedom for reporters at the local newspaper, appropriate questions to ask about members of your future audience might include the following:

- How many of my audience members will be fellow reporters?

- Will editors and publishers be present?

- What are likely to be the attitudes about greater freedom for reporters among the editors and publishers?

- Will certain opinion leaders among the management group of the paper be present? If so, what are their opinions about greater freedom for reporters?

Questions of this kind should enable you to make an educated estimate of the attitudes and needs of the particular audience you will be facing. Once you know those attitudes and needs you can begin planning your persuasive strategy.

Using Different Approaches for Different Audiences

As you might guess, the strategies a persuasive speaker uses for each audience type are as different as the audiences are. Following is an overview of the approaches and strategies you might consider for each audience type.

APPROACHING A POSITIVE AUDIENCE. For the positive audience, your job is a relatively easy one—keep them happy or make them even happier! Since the positive audience is already in basic agreement with you, you have probably been invited to speak either to rededicate or remotivate them or to talk about means rather than ends. A common example of a speaker facing a positive audience is that of a coach giving a pep talk to a team before the big game. The team members form a positive audience in the sense that they share the same goal as the coach—they all want to win. The coach's job as a speaker, then, is not to convince them that they should win but to "psyche them up" and convince them that certain tactics will work better than others in achieving the win. Speeches of this kind, given to positive audiences, are sometimes referred to as inspirational speeches.

APPROACHING A NEUTRAL AUDIENCE. The neutral audience needs information. Certain kinds of information, especially factual information, can be convincing in itself, particularly when fact is piled upon fact. The strategy for handling a neutral audience, then, is one of presenting the listeners with information from which they can reach only one conclusion—the conclusion you want them to reach. William Norris shows how to apply this strategy in his speech about reducing unemployment and underemployment:

> The requirements for effecting long-term solutions to these problems are reasonably clear. To prevent unemployment from becoming even more critical over the next decade, we must create close to 20 million new jobs. To increase the overall productivity of the labor force, we must emphasize the creation of skilled jobs. To reduce both structural unemployment and underemployment, we must upgrade the training and skills of workers. The only way to achieve these goals is through a comprehensive full employment program.

Notice how the speaker used specific examples and solutions. In this manner, he increased his chances of persuading his audience to agree that the goals need to be achieved.

APPROACHING A DISINTERESTED AUDIENCE. Facing a disinterested audience is harder than facing a neutral one. When an audience is aware of an issue but considers it unworthy of any mental strain on their part or too dull to bother getting excited about, the speaker's main persuasive task is somehow to light a fire under those listeners. Often this can be done by shocking the audience into understanding how the topic directly affects them. James B. Hayes, Publisher Emeritus of *Fortune* magazine, used this technique when appealing to his listeners about the need to reach out to at-risk youth:

> There has always been child abuse, but never as much as now. There has always been drug abuse, but never as much as now. There have always been kids with guns, kids dropping out, kids without hope. But never, ever as many as there are today in America. . . . [W]e are asking business to lead this revolution and energize all Americans to save the American dream for future generations. . . .
>
> One of the major reasons for focusing on business is that business is uniquely positioned to take action. But most importantly, business has the practical vested interest—the children of today are the workers and the customers of tomorrow. They are the future of the American business community. Business has the resources and the organizational know-how to actually *do* something about it.

APPROACHING AN OPPOSED AUDIENCE. Dealing with an opposed audience can be tougher yet. Lee Iacocca has this recollection about giving a speech to a tough audience:

> When I told the American Bar Association in 1987 that lawyers were inflicting grievous harm on the country and they should be more responsible in using our courts to distribute justice instead of redistributing wealth, I didn't know whether they would applaud me or pelt me with tomatoes. Fortunately, they applauded, and did it on their feet. The truth may sometimes hurt, but there's always a market for it if it's sold right.

Facing an audience that does not share your view requires a double strategy. First, the listeners must be "softened up" to the point where they will really listen to your arguments and consider them fairly. Second, you must present sound evidence to back your position. Imagine that you have discovered some shady dealings during your union's most recent election for officers. As a leader in your union, you plan to expose these practices in an upcoming speech, to be titled "Whatever Happened to Integrity?" You know you will face an opposed audience, since most of the members of your union were very active and involved in the elections process either as candidates or campaign workers. Starting your speech with a direct attack on the issue, like the one below, would be an almost certain way to lose that kind of audience right at the beginning:

> Union politics at this company are riddled with graft and corruption. The recent election showed me quite clearly that we cannot trust either the winners or the losers. In an election where vote-buying occurred and campaign workers tampered with ballot boxes . . .

Such an opening will only deepen the negative feelings of an opposed audience. Even with facts to back up your claims, it is unlikely that you would achieve a fair hearing for your case. A better approach for this kind of audience would be the following:

> This union has always had good leadership. I think you will agree that during our years here we have been fortunate in the people we have elected as our officers and stewards. I know many of you are proud of this union and want to see it succeed. So I was very surprised and shocked recently to discover some irregularities in our recent election process. Please listen as I recount some facts that have come to my attention. . . .

This approach may not persuade your listeners to believe you any more than they would have with the first approach, but at least in the second case your audience is more likely to listen to your arguments and consider them. If the arguments you then present in the body of the speech are strong enough, the listeners may be persuaded.

APPROACHING A MIXED AUDIENCE. Of course, positive, neutral, disinterested, and opposed audiences do not always occur in pure form. Many times an audience is composed of people who disagree amongst themselves. When an audience is made up of positive listeners and neutral listeners, the speaker's task is not too difficult. Giving persuasive information to such a group satisfies the neutral listeners and recharges those who already agree. You can use the same approach effectively with an audience of neutral and opposed listeners, but it should be preceded in this case by some "mind-opening" tactics before presenting the factual information. For a disinterested and opposed group, the approach suggested for opposed listeners alone may prove effective. Perhaps the worst combination to face is an audience of positive and opposed listeners. Here, too, the safest approach might be to use the strategy for opposed listeners. By appealing mainly to them, you may gain some converts from your opposed listeners and are unlikely to lose any of the positive ones. Specific kinds of evidence that can be useful in dealing with these different types of audiences will be presented later in this chapter.

ETHOS: ESTABLISHING YOUR PRESTIGE

Recall from Chapter 5 that Aristotle used the term *ethos* to describe a speaker's prestige. He felt it was the most powerful form of proof a speaker could possess. No matter how well a speaker appeals to the needs of the listeners, no matter how logical the speaker, if the listeners do not respect the speaker's character, there is little chance of successful persuasion. Accordingly, to be an effective speaker, you must establish *ethos,* especially when attempting to persuade an opposed audience. This is done by showing listeners you are well-prepared and competent, sincere in what you say, and genuinely interested in your audience.

Showing Competence and Preparedness

Only speakers who know their topic thoroughly and feel confident in their preparation are likely to succeed in persuading their listeners. If you are frightened or hesitant, or if your preparation has been shallow or haphazard, you will find it almost impossible to convince your audience of anything. Abraham Lincoln's well-known saying applies aptly to persuasive speaking: "You can fool some of the people all of the time, and all of the people some of the time, but you cannot fool all of the people all of the time." Incompetence and lack of confidence will usually become obvious to most audiences after a short period of time.

While audiences seldom fail to notice incompetence, they may occasionally fail to recognize a truly competent speaker. If no one points out a speaker's knowledge, preparation, and ability to the listeners, they may misjudge the true qualities of that speaker. Sometimes a speaker's qualifications are mentioned in a prespeech introduction. Other times, the speaker has already established a national reputation in a given field or is well known to a local audience, in which case it is unnecessary to remind listeners of the speaker's competence. Unfortunately, the speakers most needing this kind of "prestige-boosting"—unknown or inexperienced speakers— are the ones who least often receive it. This leaves them with the task of building their own *ethos* during their speeches. Ethos-building can be accomplished in a number of ways, including letting your speech preparation do the talking for you, referring to your own experiences with the topic, or by more overtly mentioning that you conducted research on the topic.

LET YOUR SPEECH PREPARATION SHOW. One of the most effective methods of assuring your audience of your competence is to let your speech preparation show during your speech. This can be accomplished in several ways. One way is by frequent use of evidence and supporting materials. The use of facts, survey results, statistics, and quotations from known authorities in the field says several important things about your knowledge and preparation. First, it assures the audience that you are not simply "putting your mouth in motion." Listeners who hear sufficient amounts of evidence will recognize that you can defend what you are saying and are not merely expressing your own unsupported opinions. Second, referring to outside sources of evidence shows the audience you have taken the time and effort to discover that evidence. Even though they may be an opposed audience, they will admire you for doing thorough research to support your point of view. They will realize you have earned the right to speak to them about your topic.

REFER TO PERSONAL EXPERIENCES. A second way of showing your competence is by referring to your own experience with your topic, particularly during the introduction of your speech. Audiences have learned to expect this kind of self-competence building from speakers and do not consider it bragging, as long as it is done in a subtle and sophisticated manner. Notice how Lee Iacocca established his competence in a speech introduction to a group of editors of in-house newspapers by referring to direct experience in their field:

> A long time ago I learned who the most powerful people in the world are: editors. And I don't just mean the editors of *The New York Times* and the *Washington Post*. I mean you people! In fact, on Friday I was visiting Lehigh University, my alma mater, and I was reminded how I first learned that lesson.
>
> I was interviewed by a bright kid from their student newspaper, the *Brown and White*. Well, I told this kid that I used to work for the paper, too . . . forty-five years ago, if you can believe that! I wasn't good enough to be the editor-in-chief, but I was the layout or makeup editor.
>
> And as the layout editor, I learned pretty quickly who has clout in the world. Most people don't have time to read stories, but they do read headlines, which I used to write. I also learned how you can turn something that's real important to somebody else into a real nothing. You just bury it on page 9. And I learned— and this was the biggest lesson of all—how easy it is to get even with people you're mad at. You just run unflattering pictures of them. That happens to me all the time!
>
> Well, I know you people are putting out some great work— and it's not just in your photo selection. I've seen some of your newsletters, and I've heard about the fact sheets, and weekly department meetings, and town hall sessions. . . . No matter how good the writing and editing is, though, I think in your business you need something more. You need credibility.

MENTION YOUR RELEVANT WORK EXPERIENCE, RESEARCH, AND SO ON. You can also show experience or preparation by mentioning a job you have had, by describing an informal survey you have taken, or simply by saying, "While researching for this speech, I noticed. . . ." So long as you do not overdo this kind of reference, your *ethos* will grow in the minds of your listeners.

Conveying Sincerity

Sincerity is the second part of a speaker's prestige. Like competence, it must be genuine to make a lasting, positive impression. Insincere speakers can impress audiences for a time, but eventually most are exposed as "fakes." What is meant by sincerity in persuasive speaking? Basically, it means that the speaker's motives for advocating a particular attitude, belief, or behavior must originate from genuine concern for the best interests of the audience rather than from self-interest.

If a politician speaks to her or his constituents about a solution to a problem during an election year, the listeners sometimes find it hard to believe that the politician is attacking the problem unselfishly. A natural question in their minds is, "Is the purpose of this speech to help solve the problem or to ensure election?" A politician speaking under such circumstances needs to make a special effort to convince the audience of her or his sincerity. Audiences will more readily accept a speaker they consider somewhat incompetent than a speaker they consider insincere. The slightest hint of insincerity will turn many listeners against a speaker instantly.

A few public speakers are gifted with *charisma*. Charisma is difficult to define, but it often enables speakers to influence and dominate their listeners in a way that ordinary speakers cannot. Charismatic speakers seem to be taken almost at face value as sincere and possessing great credibility. They are highly captivating and can often carry their audiences away with their words. Because they wield such power over their listeners, speakers who possess this gift have a special responsibility to use it wisely. To use it for the wrong purposes not only harms the particular audiences that hear such a speaker; it also breaks down the trust that must exist between speakers and listeners everywhere if persuasion is to continue to be a means by which decisions are made in a democratic society.

Establishing Good Will

Audiences will be more open and receptive to a speaker who shows an interest in them or good will toward them. Particularly with opposed audiences, persuaders need first to open the minds of their listeners to secure a fair hearing for their side of the issue. Getting an audience to like you as a person can lead to its members liking and accepting your arguments.

EXPRESS APPRECIATION FOR THE INVITATION TO SPEAK. One commonly used method of showing an interest in one's audience is the practice of expressing appreciation for the invitation to speak to the group. Indeed, the first order of business for many speakers is to voice an appreciation for the privilege of addressing the audience. This can be accomplished by simply saying thank you at the outset of your speech: "Thank you for inviting me to spend some time with you this evening," or "Good afternoon. It is a real pleasure to be here with you today."

COMPLIMENT THE AUDIENCE. Closely related to thanking one's audience is complimenting them. If you genuinely believe "This club represents the leaders in our community," then do not hesitate to tell the club that. If you consider your audience to be a fair-minded group of people with sound judgment, tell them that as well—especially if your topic is likely to demand that they be fair as they listen: "This group has a reputation for being open-minded and fair in its decisions. I feel confident you will listen to what I have to say today in that same spirit." An opening such as this compliments the listeners and also challenges them to be fair-minded as they listen to your speech.

SPEAK DIRECTLY TO INDIVIDUALS. Another way to show interest in your audience is to speak directly to individuals in the group. If you are well acquainted with members of your audience, you may want to call them by name during your introductory remarks: "I see my friend Charles Stevens here today. I'm glad you could be here, Charlie." This sort of public recognition flatters the person and probably puts him in a more receptive frame of mind toward you and your message. But calling audience members by name can be risky. If you call one friend's name, you'd better call all of your friends by name; otherwise, those left out may feel slighted. If you see twenty-eight of your friends in the audience, you'd better avoid such a roll call altogether! Take care also not to identify someone as a friend if that person is only a nodding acquaintance. This comes across as false and insincere.

IDENTIFY COMMON GROUND. To show interest in your audience in another way, you might identify interests and experiences you and your listeners have in common. The use of the common ground technique is a good method for demonstrating a genuine interest in your listeners as people. Audiences appreciate this.

USE HUMOR. Effective use of humor also makes the speaker seem a likable person. If you can make your listeners laugh with you, they are more likely to listen receptively to your serious, persuasive message.

LOGOS: PRESENTING YOUR ARGUMENT LOGICALLY

Have you ever been in an argument with someone and found yourself saying, "You're not being logical!" If you have, you probably still remember how frustrated you felt because the other person wouldn't argue according to the rules of logic. People frequently make decisions based on their needs and desires, but they like to feel they have decided logically. A persuasive speaker's job is to show listeners through logic how to fulfill their needs and desires. Like *pathos* and *ethos, logos* is a powerful tool for the effective persuasive speaker. The three primary means of achieving good logic are to use valid evidence and correct reasoning, make your evidence suit your audience, and use a logical framework.

Using Valid Evidence and Correct Reasoning

Being logical in persuasive speaking means using valid evidence and correct reasoning. Evidence is the raw material with which you must begin. Reasoning is the process of putting this raw material together into a logical argument, which in turn may be used to reach a logical conclusion. The process of building a logical argument for use in a persuasive speech can be compared to the way mighty rivers are formed: Rivers begin in the mountains and hills in tiny rivulets and creeks (evidence), which then flow together (the reasoning process) to form larger streams. Finally, these larger streams come together as a mighty river (the conclusion).

As an example, imagine that your task is to persuade your fellow townspeople that your community desperately needs a new hospital. To reach this conclusion, you must begin with the various types of evidence we discussed in Chapter 2: facts, statistics, testimony, narrative, examples, and comparisons. The most persuasive evidence you can use generally consists of facts or statistics. Testimony, when the opinions are based upon facts, is also a very persuasive type of evidence. On the topic of the new hospital, an example of evidence might be, "Twenty-four people who could not get beds in our present hospital died last year." Another might be, "Neighboring Jamestown has twice the number of hospital beds that we have to fill the same level of need."

Once you have chosen your evidence, use the process of reasoning to make sure that the evidence flows together logically to produce the conclusion you wish to reach. If your conclusion is based on three arguments but you have supported only one of them with evidence, you will have difficulty convincing your audience to agree with you. If your evidence is weak or contrary to the practical experience of the audience, you are again likely to fail. To succeed, your reasoning must show how each piece of evidence works with the other pieces of evidence, how all of them together lead to one very definite conclusion—the conclusion you wish the audience to reach.

Making Your Evidence Suit Your Audience

Certain forms of evidence are especially suitable for certain kinds of audiences. Let's return to our four basic types of audiences—the positive audience, the neutral audience, the disinterested audience, and the opposed audience. Which kinds of evidence do you suppose work best with each of these audience types?

The positive audience needs recharging, not convincing. Therefore, anecdotes, examples, and comparisons seem most effective with such listeners. Recall that neutral audiences lack information about the topic—they need information that will make it possible for them to form an opinion. As such, while examples are helpful, facts, statistics, and testimony will stand a better chance. The disinterested audience must be given facts and statistics, too. They must be shown that a serious problem exists, or is about to become critical, and that it affects them. The opposed audience needs all the tools at the speaker's command. With an opposed audience, the speaker is wise to start with humor, common ground devices, or compliments. An anecdote can also work well at the beginning. Once the listeners have decided to give the speaker a fair hearing, these can be followed with the harder forms of evidence (facts, statistics, examples, and comparisons). Correct reasoning is important no matter what type of audience you face. Logical reasoning is especially important, however, when facing an opposed audience. Often, of course, your listeners will be mixed in their needs and attitudes. These groups react best when the speaker analyzes their needs correctly, then applies the various kinds of evidence in the best proportions.

Using a Logical Framework

Two of the speech patterns discussed earlier provide an especially logical framework for persuasive speeches. These are the problem-solution pattern and Monroe's Motivated Sequence. Before you continue, you may want to review these organizational patterns in Chapter 2. Both offer certain ideas that may be useful in developing a logical strategy for your persuasive speeches.

Whichever pattern you use, your persuasive speeches must have an introduction, a body, and a conclusion. While these three basic parts of a speech serve similar functions in almost every speech type, each requires a particular point of emphasis in persuasive speeches. First, in the introduction you must be certain to build your *ethos*. In the body, it is essential to use valid evidence and correct reasoning. In the conclusion, you must reestablish your *ethos* and clearly indicate the response you desire from your audience.

BEING RESPONSIBLE

Persuasive speaking is one of the major ways in which decisions are reached in a free society. The President of the United States attempts to persuade the American public to adopt a plan for warding off inflation. Business leaders work constantly to persuade customers to buy. Citizens have the opportunity to persuade each other to vote for a particular candidate in each election. A speaker who can persuade effectively sometimes wields great influence over the minds of others. But with this influence comes responsibility.

Centuries ago, the Roman rhetorician Quintilian defined the ideal orator as "a good man skilled in speaking." In doing so, he placed major focus on good character as the primary requirement for effective persuasive speaking. Being a responsible persuader does not guarantee you will always be right in what you advocate to an audience, but it does mean you honestly believe you are right. If you try to convince consumers to buy your product, for example, you should sincerely believe that product is right for their needs and desires, not simply be trying to meet a sales quota. If you are asking a group of people to vote for you, you should genuinely be convinced that you are the best-qualified candidate and not wish simply to increase your own personal power.

Responsible persuasion can mean different things to different people. For centuries, however, most persuaders have agreed on certain ethical standards without which the process of persuasion loses much of its value. At the top of the list is the belief that any form of deception is wrong. We can translate that credo into a list of don'ts:

- Don't present false evidence.
- Don't present the ideas of others as if they were your own.
- Don't appeal to the emotions of your listeners without any basis in fact.
- Don't pose as an authority if you are not.

These forms of deception are considered both irresponsible and unethical. Responsible persuasion means telling the truth as you have discovered it.

CHAPTER SEVEN

Special Kinds of Speaking

"Ladies and gentlemen, it is my great pleasure and distinct honor to introduce. . . ." "How do I find the words to thank you adequately, my friends and co-workers for so many years. . . ." "On behalf of our entire management team, we are pleased to present you with this plaque honoring your extraordinary service. . . ." Each of these lines comes from special-situation speeches given every day—speeches of introduction, speeches of acceptance, commemorative speeches. Although less common than informative and persuasive speeches, special-situation speeches are no less important. Professionally and personally, you may be asked on many occasions to introduce a speaker, express a public thank you for a gift, honor a fellow worker who is leaving, or deliver a keynote address. Although you will find elements of informing and persuading in nearly all of these special-situation speeches, their primary purpose is not necessarily to inform or persuade. Instead, their chief purpose, typically, is to inspire, to challenge, to honor, to entertain—in short, to make us feel good about ourselves and those around us.

And just as the purpose of these speeches differs from that of informative and persuasive speeches, so do the skills they require. All of the skills we have discussed thus far in the book—researching, finding supporting materials, organizing the speech, building *ethos,* and the like—certainly remain important. However, in most speeches for special situations, your principal focus should be your language usage, memory, and delivery skills. Vivid language is important to inspire the audience and to make the speech occasion a celebration. Well-chosen words help you highlight the formality and seriousness of most special-situation speeches. Memorizing brief but key portions of these speeches also adds impact to your delivery.

In this final chapter, we will discuss special-situation speeches and their particular nuances. First, we will look at speeches that focus on people, such as introductions, acceptances, and testimonials, then speeches for special occasions, such as keynote addresses and dedications. Last comes a section on impromptu speaking, which, although it is more a method of speaking than a speech type, certainly deserves some attention. Examples of each special occasion speech type, as well as examples of informative and persuasive speeches, are provided in the Appendix, which immediately follows this chapter.

SPEAKING THAT FOCUSES ON PEOPLE

Has it ever occurred to you to ask yourself as you sat through what seemed an unending keynote address at a convention or a tedious commencement speech, "Why do we bother with such speeches at all?" Indeed, they can seem endless and boring to those not heavily involved with the convention or graduation. But when it is your spouse being honored or it is your own graduation ceremony, the speech usually means a great deal more. In short, we honor those who have achieved great things because we value what they have accomplished. We could conceivably hand a terrific swimming coach who is retiring a watch or a plaque without saying a word. That would honor the coach to some extent, but a public speech accompanying the plaque makes it an occasion. The coach is more fittingly thanked with the gift and the speech, and those who hear the speech are again reminded of the importance of those qualities the coach showed toward her swimmers—kindness, patience, leadership, and concern.

There are several speech types that focus on people. Here we will focus on those given most frequently: speeches of introduction, speeches of presentation, speeches of acceptance, and commemorative speeches honoring people. We will discuss the purpose of each of these kinds of speeches and offer some guidelines for delivering them.

Learning about Speeches of Introduction

Speeches of introduction are intended to say to the audience, "You will benefit from listening to this speaker." They should also tell the speaker, "This audience is anxious to hear your speech." However, the two major purposes facing someone who introduces a guest speaker are actually to build enthusiasm for the guest speaker by establishing his or her credibility and to build audience interest in the guest speaker's topic. Too often those giving speeches of introduction make little or no preparation and simply read a few lines from a speaker's résumé to the audience. Such an approach does little to fulfill either of the basic purposes and cheats both the guest speaker and the audience. Following a few guidelines when preparing a speech of introduction can make a tremendous difference.

First, keep speeches of introduction brief—typically from thirty seconds to three minutes, depending on how well-known the speaker already is to the audience. Second, be accurate in every detail of your introduction. Start with your pronunciation of the speaker's name. Nothing can more surely destroy the impact of an otherwise superb speech of introduction than to mispronounce the main speaker's name. If you think you might forget it, have it in front of you in writing. If it is a difficult name to pronounce, be certain to learn the correct pronunciation beforehand, then practice it. Also, be sure that you know the basic facts about the speaker's background. Since speeches of introduction are brief, you should have no problems with memory. However, if you think there is a chance you may forget an important fact or reverse the order of some facts, bring a brief outline on a note card with you to the podium.

Next, suit your level of formality to the occasion. You would obviously be more formal and restrained in your introduction of the CEO of your worldwide organization than you would be in introducing a fellow employee from your office to roast your local manager. Your language would undoubtedly be more formal and serious in the first case, as would the whole tone of your introduction. For the roast, on the other hand, a more informal approach would be appropriate.

Make the speaker you are introducing feel good. Not only are you trying to generate enthusiasm in the audience, you also want your introduction to serve as a springboard from which the speaker can launch into an inspiring speech. Be factual about his or her accomplishments and show how the speaker's background and experience have prepared him or her to speak with authority on this topic. Be wary of overdoing it, though. Don't embarrass the speaker with excessive praise. Be especially careful not to praise his or her speaking skills—telling the audience that they are about to hear one of the great orators of the last decade starts the main speaker off with little or no chance of succeeding.

Also, don't reveal personal incidents of the speaker's life that could be embarrassing. Sometimes this is done in an attempt to get a laugh, as in: "Why, I've known Seth Mobley since he was the dumbest kid in the fifth grade. How he ever managed to become a lawyer is still a mystery to me!" The audience may laugh, but Seth won't come to the podium feeling good about himself and his speech.

The introduction should also show the listeners the relationships among the speaker's background, the chosen topic, and the audience's interests. An introduction that simply lists the accomplishments of the speaker and stops fails to fulfill its basic purpose. What each audience member wants to know from an introducer is, "Why will this speaker, speaking on this topic, be interesting to me?" A competent introducer shows why the speaker's background qualifies him or her to speak on this particular topic, and why it will prove interesting to this particular audience. Too often an introducer fails to discover in advance what topic the speaker plans to talk about. This makes it difficult to tie the speaker's topic and the audience's interests together. The wise introducer always checks with the main speaker several days before the speech occasion to learn not only what the topic will be, but what approach the speaker plans to take.

Finally, an introducer should work to build a feeling of expectation and drama among the members of the audience. Speeches of introduction are similar to an appetizer before a meal—both tease the taste buds in anticipation of the main course to come. Probably the most common technique for building expectation in speeches of introduction is to save the name of the main speaker until the end of the introduction in order to make it the high point. When most of the audience already knows the speaker, the introducer should concentrate instead on imparting little-known facts about the speaker's background, especially those that relate to her or his knowledge and expertise on the topic.

Generating a sense of expectation and drama requires a well-rehearsed speech of introduction. Many introducers neglect to rehearse—even a single time—because they are "just the introducer." The brevity of speeches of introduction seems to lull many people into a false sense of preparedness. Although there is indeed little chance of forgetting such a short speech, the effectiveness of speeches of introduction relies on language usage, memory, and delivery factors. Regardless of brevity, each of these skills requires thorough rehearsal.

Understanding Speeches of Presentation

Frequently when someone receives a gift or award, a speech of presentation accompanies it. Typical examples include the countless occasions when gifts are presented to friends or colleagues who are moving, retiring, or completing a term in elective office. The primary purpose of a speech of presentation is, of course, to honor the recipient. When necessary, secondary purposes can include explaining the purpose for which an award is being given and praising the losers in cases where there has been competition for an award.

Speeches of presentation are short, usually lasting no more than four or five minutes. In delivering very brief speeches of just one or two minutes—for example, when presenting a gift—the presenter typically asks the recipient to stand near the podium during the presentation speech so he or she can immediately receive the award. During longer speeches of presentation, the recipient remains seated until the speech is completed, then approaches the podium to accept the award or gift. Additionally, as in speeches of introduction, the presenter should take care not to overpraise and risk embarrassing the recipient. It is usually best to restrict your remarks primarily to the actions or qualities of the recipient for which the award is being given.

In an often-used pattern of organization for a speech of presentation, the presenter satisfies three goals:

1. Describing the award and reading any engraved message with which the audience is not familiar.
2. Indicating the values the award attempts to honor.
3. Showing how the actions and character of the recipient reflect those values.

The order of these three goals may vary. Many presenters intertwine a description of the values with a recounting of the actions and character of the recipient. Moreover, depending on the situation, the description of the award may come first or last. No matter what pattern of organization is used, however, remember that the chief purpose of a speech of presentation is to honor the recipient.

Giving Speeches of Acceptance

If you have watched such ceremonies as the Academy Awards, the Emmys, or the Tonys on television, you know that acceptance speeches can take many forms and can vary in length from a simple "thank you" to a lengthy monologue. In their ideal form, however, speeches of acceptance have the direct purpose of thanking both those bestowing the award and those who helped the recipient gain it.

Whenever you think there is a reasonable chance that you might receive a gift or award, prepare a brief speech of acceptance in advance. Be certain to thank everyone involved in both presenting and helping you attain the award. You may also modestly mention your commitment and that of others to the values and actions for which the award is given, but place the focus on the values and actions, not on yourself. Unless it is clear that the award is expected to serve as the introduction for a major speech, keep acceptance speeches to no more than two or three minutes. Most audiences respond favorably to a speech of acceptance, provided it is brief. Bear in mind, too, that an acceptance speech is given for the audience's benefit. It is an acknowledgment that the award has been accepted and appreciated.

Sometimes you will be taken by surprise by the presentation of an award. When that happens, you have no choice but to speak impromptu, a skill we will address at the end of this chapter. If you have any doubt whether or not you are expected to give a speech when accepting an award, ask the presenter for advice.

Practicing Commemorative Speeches

Commemorative speeches remain among the most inspiring and best remembered in our country's history. Abraham Lincoln's Gettysburg Address, Edward Kennedy's speech at his brother Robert's funeral, and Ronald Reagan's speech following the *Challenger* disaster served to implant the memory of brave people in our minds and to inspire us to reach for the ideals for which they stood. Though commemorative speeches sometimes recall events rather than persons, here we will look at those that are focused exclusively on persons—testimonial speeches and eulogies.

TESTIMONIAL SPEECHES. Testimonial speeches are given to honor living persons. Their purpose is to praise someone or to celebrate an occasion focused around persons. You may hear testimonial speeches given in the form of speeches of farewell and appreciation when a boss or co-worker is moving away, as roasts for those successful and well-liked in their careers, or as toasts at weddings and retirement dinners. They may range in length from a toast of a few seconds to a roast with a dozen or more speakers taking from five to ten minutes each to honor an individual with tongue-in-cheek humor. Most often they are given in connection with a dinner, or at least when food is being served—at a wedding reception, for example.

The testimonial speaker deals in feelings, not facts. He or she tries to stir emotions, not thoughts. Though the speaker may narrate some scenes from the life of the person being honored, the purpose is to generate respect, admiration, appreciation, and best wishes for the future. The speaker will evoke joy, laughter, celebration, and sentiment from the audience while honoring the special person.

Testimonial speakers depend heavily on the creative use of language. If an informative speaker can be compared with an essayist, the testimonial speaker is like a poet. A good testimonial speaker chooses language rich in connotation and steeped in emotion to create a warm and positive mood fitting the occasion.

When humor is used, as is the case at roasts, its purpose should always be to honor the individual for whom the roast is given. Occasionally speakers at roasts, keen on getting laughs from the audience, will relate a funny incident that is truly embarrassing. Such an approach does not honor the person. To the contrary, it usually harms the speaker's image in the audience's eyes, even though the listeners will laugh at the joke. If you are asked to speak at a roast, pick humor that you know will genuinely amuse the roastee as well as the audience. If you have any doubts, either ask the roastee privately beforehand or skip that particular story.

EULOGIES. Eulogies are commemorative speeches given to honor those who have died. Although they are most often delivered at a funeral service, they may be given weeks, months, or even years later. As with testimonial speeches, the purpose of eulogies is to honor and praise an individual. An equally important purpose of eulogies is to comfort and uplift the listeners who feel the loss of a loved one or a great person. The eulogist has a difficult task, since emotions of sorrow and loss are usually high among the audience. The eulogist must respect those feelings, while at the same time attempting to inspire those present by recounting the virtues of the deceased.

The eulogist typically picks out several of the most noble and praiseworthy attributes of the deceased and extols them with examples from the person's life. The eulogist may also call upon the listeners to remember and imitate those virtues. However, the essence of a eulogy is to honor the person who has died.

As with testimonial speeches honoring the living, the most important tool for the eulogist is lofty language. Great care must be taken to select words and phrases that are noble, dignified, and moving. Because the eulogy depends so much on eloquent language, it is often written in advance, then delivered from manuscript or memory. Experienced speakers will occasionally use a combination of read, memorized, and extemporaneous delivery with excellent effect.

Providing Speeches for Special Occasions

Various kinds of public occasions are highlighted by speeches. Large meetings and conventions, dedication ceremonies, and some public lectures employ a speech as a focal point of the event. Generally, the purpose of such speeches is to commemorate the meeting or ceremony that is taking place. In this section, we will look briefly at three kinds of special occasion speeches: keynote speeches, dedication speeches, and public relations speeches.

Delivering Keynote Speeches

Meetings or conventions of many large organizations begin with a keynote speech. Most Americans are familiar with the keynote addresses delivered near the opening of the Democratic and Republican conventions every four years. In addition to these political speeches, keynote addresses occur regularly at business and professional conventions ranging from those of the American Medical Association to those of the National Council of Teachers of English.

Keynote speeches serve several purposes. First, they rally the members of the organization around its central goals and purposes. Since such large organizations typically meet only once a year, the keynote address opens each new convention by renewing the enthusiasm and commitment of the membership to its values and purposes. Second, they provide a common theme or focus for the particular meeting that year. The speaker will sometimes need to stress the specific goals and issues facing the organization in the upcoming year. On other occasions the need may be to sound a call for unity, particularly if the organization is threatening to splinter apart. Still other circumstances may demand that the keynote address focus on a crisis facing the organization and stress the importance of this year's convention in meeting it. Finally, since a keynote speech usually provides the central focus for a convention, it also commemorates it. Such speeches later come to stand for the themes or highlights of past conventions.

The keynote speaker is usually a well-respected member of the organization or some well-known person from the outside who has great credibility with the members. The keynote speaker's job is that of a cheerleader, molding the members into an enthusiastic and involved group.

Giving Dedication Speeches

The word *dedication* has several dictionary definitions, including: "To set apart for any special use, duty, or purpose"; "To commit (oneself) to a certain course of action or thought"; "To open or unveil (a bridge, statue, etc.) to the public." Thus cities dedicate new city halls, schools, or parks; citizens dedicate the opening of the annual United Way fund drive; and clubs dedicate their founding.

Public speeches make up the major part of dedication ceremonies. They serve to highlight the meaning of a new creation that is being dedicated or a new endeavor that is being started. The dedication speaker focuses the listeners' attention on the goals and values that the new creation (building, piece of art work) represents or that the new endeavor stands for. The length of dedication speeches may vary, depending mainly on the scope of the new creation or endeavor and on the expectations of audience. Sometimes only one speaker will address those gathered for the ceremony; at other times there will be a series of briefer speeches.

When dedicating a new hospital, for example, a speaker might briefly outline the history of the building project and mention the names of key board members and administrators whose vision and planning resulted in the completed structure in which the audience is now seated. The speaker's main thrust, however, would be to stress what the new hospital will mean to the city and the region in the future. In that vein, the speaker might note the importance of physical well-being in today's society, then paint a picture of the thousands who will regain their health in the facility over the next half century.

As with other speeches for special occasions, the speaker's success depends largely on clear and lofty language, memorization of key passages, and a direct and dynamic delivery.

Presenting Public Relations Speeches

Today, business and industry spend a great amount of time and money on image building, or public relations. They do it not only through television, but also by regularly sending their executives out on the lecture circuit. Carl Terzian, a consultant in executive speech training has noted that:

> A growing number of executives not only are enthusiastically acknowledging lecture requests, but are actually seeking them out. Influencing others is very rewarding. Some employ the platform to champion the cause of industry; to create a healthier business climate; to generate sales; to proclaim ambitious corporate goals; [or] to promote an image. . . .

In addition to corporations' increasing use of public relations speeches, government services and educational institutions are also using this approach to maintain contact with the public and to promote a positive image.

Unlike the other special-occasion speeches we have looked at, the public relations speech has a strong persuasive purpose. That purpose is not to sell a particular product or a specific service, however. Instead, the purpose is to promote an overall positive image of the organization. Such speeches often include a broad informative purpose as well, since promoting a positive image frequently demands giving the listeners facts about one's company.

A public relations speaker typically makes three general points:

1. Outlining the goals and purposes of the organization.
2. Showing the audience how those goals tie in with their needs and values.
3. Indicating how the organization can help people.

At times, the public relations speaker may not only represent his or her own organization but an entire group of similar organizations. For example, the speaker who works for a national retail chain may address the question: "How can large retail chains recapture the spirit of the old country store?" Such a topic does not directly promote the company's products or the products of other retailers, but it does help the consumer in the audience see giant chains as reaching for a more personal, down-home brand of service.

PRACTICING IMPROMPTU SPEAKING

The types of speeches for special occasions mentioned so far in this chapter are just that—*types* of speeches. Impromptu speaking, on the other hand, is a *method* of speaking—a way of delivering any kind of speech. In Chapter 4, we compared impromptu speaking with manuscript, memorized, and extemporaneous delivery methods. We called it the kind of delivery one must use when asked to speak with no advance notice and with only a moment or two in which to prepare. In reality, you speak impromptu each time your manager asks you to tell the group your opinion in the midst of a meeting or when you stand up and respond to an important point at a public gathering. Sometimes you can do so informally, from your seat; at other times you will be expected to stand or even to speak from a podium.

Whatever the situation, the first rule to keep in mind is *don't panic!* When you recall that you have delivered impromptu remarks in the past, you can have confidence in your ability to speak off the cuff to large groups. Audiences don't expect impromptu speeches to be polished orations—they just want to hear your thoughts spoken in whatever words come to you at the moment. They also do not expect to hear a lengthy impromptu speech. Listeners are nearly always sympathetic with public speakers, no matter whether they have had time for preparation or not. They are especially understanding toward those speaking impromptu.

Although your flow of words may not be as smooth when speaking impromptu as you would prefer, you can manage to sound well-organized. Here is a simple three-step plan of organization that will help you collect and present your thoughts. You can apply it to most impromptu speaking situations:

1. State the point you are answering (if you have been asked to respond to a previous speaker). Or state the main point you wish to make. You need not elaborate on your point.

2. Support the main point with appropriate examples, statistics, and testimony.

3. Summarize and restate your main point. (If your speech has been less than a minute in length, you may want to omit this step.)

Many of the impromptu "speeches" you are asked to give are really brief "statements" during parliamentary meetings or in smaller groups. When someone asks a question and you feel the urge to respond, your answer, however brief, is an impromptu speech. More formal occasions may call for more formal delivery and perhaps a longer speech, but they are essentially no different than your answer in the meeting. Use the many opportunities that arise to give brief impromptu responses, taking advantage of the three-step organizational pattern suggested above. Then, when you are asked to give a longer impromptu speech, you will be familiar with the basic method.

Model Speeches

Speech to Inform

Successful Strategies for Achieving Your Career Goals
Write Them, Review Them, Achieve Them

Virgis Colbert, Vice-President, Plant Operations, Miller Brewing Company

Delivered to the Southeastern Wisconsin Black MBA Planning Council, Milwaukee, Wisconsin, September 21, 1993

Thank you for inviting me to spend some time with you this evening. As requested, I'd like to share some thoughts with you on "Successful Strategies for Achieving Your Career Goals."

Someone once asked James Lofton, wide-receiver for the Buffalo Bills, what tricks he used to achieve success. Lofton replied,

> One trick is to work harder than the other guy. The second trick, always hustle, Third trick, study and know what you're doing. Fourth trick, always be prepared. Fifth, never give up. Those are my tricks.

What Lofton was really saying is that there are no "tricks" for getting ahead, but there are some very basic fundamentals of hard work and planning that can give each of us a competitive edge, if we use them.

I believe one of the most important fundamentals is the importance of setting goals. If I had to boil my advice about goals down to one short set of three bullet points, I'd say:

- First, set very specific goals;
- Second, write down those goals; and
- Third, review them and work toward their accomplishment on a daily basis.

Let's review those three points very quickly.

The first point is to set very specific goals. Someone once defined a goal as "a dream with a deadline."

Many people have high ambitions and want to achieve success, but they never get around to defining specifically what they want to achieve, what specific position they want to fill, or what specific expertise they want to develop that will set them apart from their competition.

A goal gives you something to aim for, and not even the greatest marksmen in the work can demonstrate their shooting skill . . . until they have a target.

A great philosopher once said that:

No wind is a fair wind if you don't know the port for which you are headed.

So strategy number one is: set a specific goal; don't be a "wandering generality." It's much more effective in life to be a "meaningful specific" than a "wandering generality."

The second strategy is to have the courage to write down your goals. Many people are afraid to actually write out their goals because they are afraid they will fail to reach them, and in later years someone else may see those goals and poke fun at them for having such high ambitions.

We should never be afraid to set high, ambitious goals.

As Ralph Waldo Emerson said:

What lies behind us, and what lies in front of us, pales in significance when compared to what lies within us.

There is a powerful, somewhat mysterious force generated when you write down your goals and frequently review them. It fixes these goals in your conscious and subconscious mind in such a way that almost everything you do will tend to move you, however slightly or subtly toward the actual realization of those goals. Things will begin to fall into place and pieces of the jigsaw puzzle of life will start to fill in the gaps.

Let me illustrate the power of the force that can be released when you write down your goals. A study of Yale University graduates in 1953 found that only 3 percent of them wrote down their goals in life. This includes actually:

- Listing their objectives;
- Setting a time limit for accomplishing each goal;
- Listing the people or organizations who could help them achieve these goals;
- Listing the obstacles that would have to be overcome;
- Spelling out what they need to know in order to achieve this goal;
- Developing a plan of action; and Spelling out why they wanted to achieve that goal.

The rest of the graduating students didn't bother to write down their goals.

Twenty years later, a follow-up study revealed that the 3 percent who had written down their goals were worth more financially than all the other 97 percent combined.

That clearly illustrates the power of written goals.

My third strategy is to review and work toward those goals on a daily basis. That enables you to see whether you are on track to achieving them or whether you need to make some adjustments.

It's like the navigator of a great ship setting off on an ocean voyage. The navigator will lay out the track on a large chart, showing all the points along which the ship is to travel. This track will be frequently updated by navigational fixes, showing where the ship actually is in relation to the desired track.

If winds and current have blown the ship off course, it is often necessary to steer ten degrees to the right or left in order to come back on track. It's the same in life, where we have to adjust our actions in order to get back on track and realize our goals.

So my first advice is to have specific goals. Goals will add focus to your life. They will create activity and generate the kind of excitement you need to realize your full potential.

Goals enable you to build a solid foundation under your dreams.

In addition to setting goals, there are some other suggestions I have that should apply regardless of whether you are in the corporate, government or academic environment.

Regardless of your profession or field of interest, demonstrate your interest in your job by knowing as much as you can about the organization you work for. As I said earlier, develop a clear set of personal objectives for your career, but stay flexible so that you can adapt yourself—and your objectives—to organizational changes.

Present yourself well. Dress appropriately and be cognizant of verbal and nonverbal mannerisms. Learn both the written and unwritten rules of the workplace. Learn how decisions for advancement are really made, and make the adjustments.

Bear in mind that it's important, although sometimes difficult, for minorities and females to distinguish between racial or gender slights and general workplace practices. You can handle these situations without giving up your dignity or your principles.

In other words, develop an understanding of the "workplace game." The business world and many areas of the public sector play hardball. This is not a kid's game!

Next, don't be ruled by your emotions. There is a perception among some people that minorities and women will operate from an emotional basis—that they wear their feelings on their sleeves. Disprove that stereotyped notion by using logical and analytical thinking to solve problems or workplace slights. Maintain a positive attitude even when it's not easy to do so.

Always think positively about yourself and your ability. If you don't, no one else will. Even more importantly, if you do, you will find that in most cases people will take you as you see yourself. If you see yourself as confident and competent, then that's the way most people are going to treat you.

Be disciplined; always strive for excellence without excuse. Set high goals for yourself, and conform to work place rules and expectations, because it all starts with you.

Become a full member of the organization. Be aware of how others perceive you in a social and professional sense. This doesn't mean that you have to brown nose, but you must make certain that you are meaningfully involved in your area of the organization.

I have already said a great deal about the importance of goals. Let me add this: set goals for yourself that are higher than those goals your employer has set for you. You'll never regret it.

You must function both as individuals and as members of a team in order to be successful in the workplace. Dr. Martin Luther King, Jr., recognized the value of teamwork. When accepting the Nobel Peace Prize in 1964, he said:

> Every time I take a flight, I am always mindful of the many people who make a successful journey possible—the known pilots and unknown ground crew.

The Nobel Prize, he said, was being given to one of the pilots, but he was accepting it on behalf of the crew.

Make an early attempt to select a mentor to provide you guidance in your career. That person need not necessarily be within your workplace. You may utilize indirect mentors by observing those individuals in your organization who are enjoying success, and you can pattern your performance after their best traits.

As African-Americans, I challenge you to accept a larger share of the responsibility for your lives. We cannot let obstacles of racism and oppression slow us down. We must overcome racism and not give in to it.

And finally I ask each of you to accept as a personal responsibility that you should give something back your community by contributing money or time to positive community initiatives. This enables you to help others as you have been helped.

There is no royal road to learning, and there is no easy path to success, but I believe that if you practice some of these strategies and techniques, you will find that they will never let you down.

I would conclude with some words from the President of the Metropolitan Milwaukee YMCA:

> Watch your thoughts; they become words.
>
> Watch your words; they become actions.
>
> Watch your actions; they become habits.
>
> Watch your habits; they become character.
>
> Watch your character; it becomes your destiny. ☐

Speech to Persuade

The New American Revolution
A Recommitment to the Needs of Our Children

James B. Hayes, Co-founder of "The New American Revolution" and Publisher Emeritus of *Fortune Magazine*

Delivered at the Town Hall Los Angeles Public Issues Forum, Los Angeles, California, February 1, 1995

I want to speak with you today about a situation in our country that has enormous impact on the future of each and every business represented in this room . . . enormous impact on the future of this community . . . enormous impact on the future of this nation.

I am speaking, of course, about the neglect of our children . . . about the neglect of our nation's greatest resource . . . about the careless neglect of our own future.

As Walfred Fassler very graciously pointed out in his introduction, for the past seven years I served very happily and proudly as the Publisher of *Fortune*. Earlier this year I stepped down from that marvelous position and, along with forty of our nation's most respected business leaders, I am doing something much more important than publishing a great magazine like *Fortune*.

I'm becoming part of a Revolution . . . a New American Revolution.

You may have already heard about it . . . or seen notice of it in *The New York Times, USA TODAY*, or any number of newspapers. We held a press conference four months ago at Public School 158 in New York City. We chose a school for the announcement because our revolution is all about children.

Our aim is nothing less than to organize the entire American business community . . . to lead the nation in a massive recommitment to the needs of our children.

Our purpose is to save the American dream for future generations . . . our slogan is "remember the future." The dream that still brings people from all over the world flocking to our shores . . . the dream that has inspired our past and shaped our present . . . I'm afraid that dream is fading from our future, because our own children no longer possess it, or even understand it.

I can personalize or pinpoint that dream to a certain extent, in an old building in East Harlem in New York City. Sometimes I think the architect must have intended it to be a slum because that's pretty much what it was when my father was born there in 1899. Back then it was just one step above a cold-water flat. And today the building still stands on the southeast corner of 122nd and Lexington Avenue. My father was born to poor immigrant parents who came to this country with nothing . . . a story heard so often.

He was a very bright young man, but after high school could not afford to go on to college so he took a job as a bookkeeper at a lumber yard in Harlem. He went to night school to become an accountant and then, without any college, went on to study law at night. He eventually became a respected attorney who argued three cases before the Supreme Court, won them all, and authored several books that became standard texts in every law school in the land. I'm telling you this because when he was born, nothing was as good as things are today. People earned less. People had less. There was far more pollution. There was certainly more disease. My father was the only one of seven children in his family to live past the age of three. But what was better was the dream.

This nation entered the 20th century full of hope . . . unbridled optimism . . . and boundless self-confidence. The editorials of the day were so up to beat you could practically set them to music. That spirit lived in that building at 122nd and Lexington. People up and down that block believed in the American dream of a better life, and they had a keen understanding of what it took to make the dream come true. Let me tell you what's in that building today. On second thought, I don't believe I have to. If you know New York City, you know what's there. There is despair. There is hopelessness, and there are not as many children playing on that street today who have a dream. For those there now, life is bleak with little or no hope of a better tomorrow.

But it is not just there that we find children who are deprived, in danger, and lacking in direction and motivation. It is everywhere across this great land of ours. Regardless of sex, race, economic status, educational level, geographic location, or any other factor, the future of this nation, its youth, is in peril. And we all know it is because it is difficult to pick up a newspaper or turn on the evening news without seeing yet again another example. For many years now the situation has been getting worse and worse.

Just this past April, two distinguished foundations, Annie E. Casey and the Carnegie Foundation both released separate reports which came to the same conclusion . . . that the well-being of children in the United States continues to deteriorate at an alarming rate by almost every standard of measurement from their living arrangements to their educational achievement to their suicide rate.

A story is told about a cross-country airline flight. One of the engines failed and the pilot shut it off and told the passengers that there was no cause for concern because the plane could fly quite well on three engines. Before long another motor began to act up. Once again, the pilot shut it down and assured the passengers that two engines were sufficient. Then a third engine stopped. Silence from the cockpit. Pretty soon the pilot appeared in the cabin. He was wearing a parachute. "Don't anyone panic," he said. "I'm going for help!"

Regarding the state of children in this country, I think it's time to panic! Think back to your own childhood. If you are over thirty, very little is the same for children today . . . with the possible exception of The Rolling Stones.

Chances are that you grew up in a two-parent household. In 1960, only 9 percent of children lived in single-parent households. Today more than 25 percent do. In 1960, 243,000 children lived with a never-married parent. By 1990, that figure was an eye-popping 5,568,000 . . . a twenty-fold increase.

Chances are pretty good that when you were a child, you felt reasonably safe in your home. Chances are pretty good that you felt safe at school. There were probably no drugs in your elementary school and certainly no guns. There was discipline in your life and rules that most people obeyed. Life was fairly predictable and it was run by adults. You had a chance to learn, to play, and to grow up with some expectation that you would in fact, grow up. Today, my friends, in many parts of the country its "Lord of the Flies" out there. Angry young people rule the streets and the halls of the schools. Greedy men use children to smuggle drugs, steal, and commit unspeakable crimes . . . even murder.

Homicide is the leading cause of death for young black men fifteen to nineteen years of age. In fact, for all children under eighteen, homicide is second only to auto accidents as the cause of death! For too many young children their lives are, as Hobbs described,

> Primitive man in a state of nature . . . their lives are solitary, poor, nasty, brutish, and short!

And in the suburbs, illegitimacy, venereal disease, crime and violence are all on the rise. Consider these few stunning facts:

- Every five seconds of the school day, a child drops out of school.
- Every fifty-five seconds a child without a high school diploma gives birth to a child.
- Every seven minutes a child is arrested on a drug offense.
- Every fourteen hours a child the age of five or younger is murdered.
- Every day 1.3 million latch key kids ages five to fourteen are left to fend for themselves for much of the day.
- Every day 135,000 children bring guns to school.
- Every day three children die of injuries inflicted by abusive parents.

All this in the most prosperous nation in the history of mankind!

There has always been child abuse, but never as much as now. There has always been drug abuse, but never as much as now. There have always been kids with guns, kids dropping outs, kids without parents, kids without love, kids committing suicide, kids without hope. But never, ever as many as there are today in America. Our children are in a state of crisis! It's time to panic! We need a crusade . . . a movement . . . yes, a revolution to save them. So we are starting one! The New American Revolution. And we are asking business to lead this revolution, and energize all Americans to save the American dream for future generations.

Why business? Because business touches every household and every individual in America. The Revolution will be led by business, but through business it will reach everyone. Why business? Because with the decline of the traditional family and the increased mobility of workers, the workplace has become the new neighborhood, the new community center. Why business? Because we can argue that with the declining influence of many traditional institutions in our society, business has become a foundation of values. As a distinguished rabbi noted, "In any free society, where wrongs exist, some are guilty . . . but all are responsible."

We want business to view the next generation as part of their responsibility! From the board rooms of the nation's largest corporations to the back rooms of main street's smallest businesses . . . from General Motors to the General Store . . . we want to create an atmosphere that encourages responsible parenting, that encourages mentoring, that encourages involvement with schools and youth activities. We want a business community culture that recognizes and rewards meaningful involvement with our young people!

By the year 2000, it is estimated that nearly two-thirds of the new entrants into the work force will be women. As women enter the work force in ever increasing numbers, child-care will become an even more complex issue. We want business to adopt a leadership role and say to their employees, "it's not just okay to take care of your kids. We insist that you take the proper care of your children." We want to challenge the business culture to make children a priority! The New American Revolution will help businesses find new ways to do this.

For instance:

- We want business to reach out to at-risk children and connect them with responsible adults. The New American Revolution will provide help and direction to facilitate this.

- We want business to increase its commitment of resources to foster existing community youth programs. Again, the New American Revolution will provide services to help them establish apprenticeship programs, mentoring programs, and others modeled on successful existing programs.

- We will serve as a clearing house or facilitator to help business make the connection with children and with the programs that serve their needs.

Somewhere out there every part of the problem is already being solved. It is up to us to find and help business understand it.

One of the major reasons for focusing on business is that business is uniquely positioned to take action. But most importantly, business has the very practical vested interest—the children of today are the workers and the customers of tomorrow. They are the future of the American business community. Business has the resources and the organizational know-how to actually do something about it. In countless cases throughout America, businesses and concerned citizens are already doing meaningful things about this problem. So much so, in fact, that I often wonder where we would be as a nation if all the wonderful work was not already being done by so many wonderful people and wonderful organizations. All across this great country many successful and innovative youth programs are already being supported and carried out by many companies. But we've got to get everybody on board!

The New American Revolution will provide information about successful programs, and act as a liaison between companies and youth-serving organizations. But programs by themselves are only part of the answer. You've heard the African adage . . . "It takes a village to raise a child." Well, if it takes a village to raise a child, then it surely takes a nation to raise a generation. While business will lead The New American Revolution, it will take everyone to win the revolution.

One of the unique and particularly powerful aspects of The New American Revolution is its breadth and sweep. It recognizes that no one single answer exists nor will any miraculous silver bullet arrive to solve all the problems of youth. The solution exists in millions of individual parts. It lies in the hearts and hands and minds of every person in this room, and in the hearts and minds of every person in America. This is like a war and it calls for a massive, national commitment. We can't leave it to the next person . . . or drop a dollar in the collection plate and say, "There, I've done my part."

Everyone . . . every single adult has to play an active role. We need to recreate the values of the old fashioned neighborhood. You know what I'm talking about. You remember the neighborhood. When I was growing up I was almost as afraid of Mrs. McConnell, the lady next door, as I was of my own mother. In those days everyone who saw a child out of line had the right to . . . indeed, was expected to nudge them back into line. By the same token, I also knew that if there was trouble I could count on Mrs. McConnell to help me . . . and the other neighbors as well. We need to create an atmosphere that pays more than lip service to our kids. We should be downright ashamed over what we've allowed to happen. We should be outraged that kids are killing kids! Outraged! We should be mad as hell because we had it all here in this country . . . we really did. We were safe. We had schools that were the envy of the world. We had children who were proud of their country. And we're letting it slip away! But it is not too late.

We need to . . . all of us need to . . . provide an atmosphere in which our children can find the reassurance of discipline and the security of love. We need to create an attitude of caring for our children in every village and town and city and suburb across this whole country. Business can serve as the catalyst to make this happen and energize the entire nation to save the dream for our children.

To galvanize America to action in this historic effort, we will launch a nationwide rally and call to action. It will be the ultimate nationwide whistle stop campaign train. At 8 a.m. on the 4th of September, the train will leave Seattle and begin a historic cross-country mission. The train will be funded and operated by The New American Revolution and on board will be a most precious cargo . . . the future of our children.

For three weeks the train will travel through the heart of America, carrying business leaders, concerned citizens, children, children's advocates, families, athletes, entertainers, and national media. With flags flying and spirits high, the train will make stops at hundreds of American towns, cities, and villages. At each stop the message will be the same:

- The time to save the American dream is now.

- The place to save it is here.
- The people to save it are us.
- We are here to begin to change the conditions that threaten our children.

As the train travels America, our goal is that every American celebrates its coming, cheers its arrival, joins its task. As the train steams eastward, we want Americans in all walks of life to be positive about participating in profound change . . . with the conviction that the future can be reclaimed . . . and the dream saved. The train concludes its mission arriving in our nation's capital on September 25, 1995.

I believe this is a national security crisis. Typically, "national security" means securing our borders from invaders and protecting our interests abroad. It calls for planning, manufacturing, sending people forth to do battle. It calls for all of us to sacrifice, to bear any burden, meet any hardship. We do it because our "national security" is threatened. We do whatever needs to be done. Historically we respond with enthusiasm because our "national security" is the highest calling of citizens. The future of this nation is at stake. Our survival is at stake! Our "national security" has never been more threatened. Our survival has never been more in question. If our descendants grow up ignorant and brutal, without a sense of their own beautiful possibilities as civilized human beings, then I foresee this country, like ancient Rome, slipping into further decadence and decline.

One hundred and fifty-seven years ago, Abraham Lincoln asked,

> At what point shall we Americans expect the approach of danger. By what means shall we fortify against it? Shall we expect some transatlantic military giant to step the ocean and crush us at a blow? Never! All the armies of Europe, Asia, and Africa combined, with all the treasure of the Earth in their military chest, with a Bonaparte for a commander, could not by force take a drink from the Ohio or make a track on the Blue Ridge in a trail of a thousand years. At what point then is the approach of danger to be expected? I answer: if it ever reach us, it must spring up amongst us . . . if destruction be our lot, we must ourselves be its author and finisher.

That was Lincoln's warning. Today, in the plight of our children, the approach of danger is upon us! You know, the Statue of Liberty is not the real name of that splendid monument in my home town. It is actually called "Liberty Enlightening the World." In so many respects we, as a nation, have done just that. For many years now, we have given the world lessons in democracy. After the Second World War, we were the most benevolent and magnanimous victors in history. We have championed peace and justice . . . fairness for all mankind. We have not been perfect, but from a historical perspective, this nation has served as a shining beacon of hope. In fact, it has been said that the most important product America has been able to produce is not the automobile or television or the computer. It is hope . . . hope.

Let us now turn inward and give that hope to our own children. We don't have all the answers, but we must begin to meet the challenge. Can we do it? Most assuredly we can if we have the will. Many years ago Sir Edward Grey likened America to a gigantic boiler:

> Once the fire is ignited under it, there is no limit to the power it can generate.

The time has come for us to light that fire! Our children need your help to light the fire under America. Won't you please join with us to save the dream for the children of America? Thank you. ☐

Speech of Introduction

Donna Teeny
A Real Trailblazer

And now I'd like to introduce to you one of the real trailblazers of women's fishing, Oregon's own Donna Teeny!

If there were a list of the top ten women in fly fishing in the world today, Donna would certainly be on it. She is not only a phenomenal steelhead, trout, and saltwater angler, she is one of America's finest instructors and destination adventure hosts as well.

But what has earned Donna a permanent place in the annals of women's legacy in the sport is the fact that she and her business partner, Rhonda Sapp of Colorado, pioneered the first full line of women's fly fishing clothing and gear under their innovative label, Dirt Roads and Damsels.

Before founding Dirt Roads and Damsels, Donna had already worked in the industry for about two decades as half of the highly regarded Teeny Nymph Company, started by her well-known husband, Jim Teeny. At the same time, Rhonda was back in Denver working behind the counter of her own fly shop. Over the years, Donna and Rhonda would get together at trade shows and lament about the fact that it was impossible to purchase fly-fishing clothing that actually fit women. So one day they decided to do something about it.

Donna is here tonight to share a bit about how she and Rhonda became the Mothers of Invention on behalf of all fly-fishing "reel women." She's an inspiration to all of us, and I know you'll enjoy what she has to say.

Without further ado, Donna Teeny! ☐

SPEECH OF PRESENTATION

PRESENTATION OF THE 1984 NOBEL PEACE PRIZE TO THE RIGHT REVEREND DESMOND MPILO TUTU

Egil Aarvik, The Nobel Committee

Delivered on December 10, 1984, in Oslo, Norway

The Norwegian Nobel Committee wishes, through the presentation of this year's Nobel Peace Prize, to direct attention to a unifying leader figure in the campaign to solve South Africa's *apartheid* problem by peaceful means. The situation as it is today is such that a peaceful solution is by no means inevitable—the repression is so brutal that a violent rebellion would be an understandable reaction. The South African has more reason now than ever before to exclaim "Cry the beloved country."

Given this situation it is all the more remarkable that human beings are able to choose a peaceful way to freedom.

It is the Nobel Committee's opinion that the means by which the South African liberation process is conducted will have wide-ranging consequences for the whole of the African continent, and therefore also for the cause of peace in the world. This is an opinion which is also expressed in a number of United Nations resolutions—most recently that passed by the Security Council in October this year. Racial discrimination in South Africa is rightly regarded as a threat to peace and as an outrageous violation of basic human rights.

Fortunately, a peaceful alternative exists. On a broad front a campaign is being fought with the weapons of the spirit and reason—a campaign for truth, freedom and justice. In recognition of the fact that it is this alternative which must succeed, the South African bishop, Desmond Tutu, has been selected as this year's Peace Prize laureate.

The contribution he has made, and is still making, represents a hope for the future, for the country's white minority as well as the black majority. Desmond Tutu is an exponent of the only form for conflict solving which is worthy of civilized nations.

It is today twenty-three years since the Nobel Peace Prize was last awarded to a South African. On that occasion it was Albert Luthuli, then president of the African National Congress, who was presented with the Prize. It is the Committee's wish that this year's award should be seen as a renewed recognition of the courage and heroic patience shown by black South Africans in their use of peaceful means to oppose the *apartheid* system. This recognition is also extended to all who, throughout the world, stand in the forefront of the campaign for racial equality as a human right.

It is unfortunately not only in South Africa that human rights are violated. Another former prizewinner, Amnesty International, informs us that such violations are known to occur in 117 countries, and that prisoners of conscience are tortured in 60 countries. Too frequently, the brutal features of power and violence mar the face of our times. But if we are willing to look for it, we can also see the face of peace—even if we have to peer through prison bars and barbed wire to find it. And, in spite of everything, new hope is raised on each occasion we see how the spirit of man refuses to be conquered by the forces of hate.

Some time ago television enabled us to see this year's laureate in a suburb of Johannesburg. A massacre of the black population had just taken place—the camera showed ruined houses, mutilated human beings and crushed children's toys. Innocent people had been murdered. Women and children mortally wounded. But, after the police vehicle had driven away with their prisoners, Desmond Tutu stood and spoke to a frightened and bitter congregation: "Do not hate," he said, "let us choose the peaceful way to freedom."

It is with admiration and humility we today present the Nobel Peace Prize to this man.

Desmond Tutu's contribution to the liberation struggle was given a special significance in 1978 when he became the first black general secretary of the South African Council of Churches. This Council of Churches is both a joint forum for the churches of South Africa and the national representative for the World Council of Churches. It includes all the major churches in the country—with the exception of the Boer Church which withdrew as a result of disagreement with the Council over the question of *apartheid*. The Catholic Church is a so-called associate member, but it is also one of the Council's strongest supporters.

As around 75 percent of all citizens of South Africa are members of the church, the body is a very representative organization. Few other organizations can make the same claim to speak for the black population.

As the dynamic leader of this Council, Desmond Tutu has formulated as his goal "a democratic and just society without racial segregation." His minimum demands are: equal civil rights for all, the abolition of the Pass Laws, a common system of education, and the cessation of the forced deportation of blacks from South Africa to the so-called "homelands."

Both through these objectives and through its practical activities the South African Council of Churches has obviously exceeded the normal scope of such an organization. The Council has become a trailblazer in the campaign for human rights, a central force in a liberation struggle and an increasingly wide-ranging support organization for the many victims of the present system's racial discrimination. Consider what happens when millions of human beings are being deported. Their homes are razed to the ground. Their personal possessions are taken from them. They lose their jobs, and are physically transported and deposited in the empty veld with just a tent and a sack of maize as their only hopes of survival.

Three million have been deported in this way, while new millions await their turn.

If we ignore for a moment the personal humiliation, the question remains—who is there to help these people to survive in their new existence? Who will help them house themselves, find water, tend to the sick or educate their children?

The system also has—obviously—its political prisoners. Their crime is the necessary one of wanting a society with freedom and respect for human rights. They are imprisoned—but who is there to help their families?

There is also the so-called "migration labor" system under which underpaid laborers are obliged to live away from their families. The Pass Laws are also notorious; they burden the black population with a collective capacity and make them foreigners in their own country. Anyone breaking these laws risks group arrest and indefinite imprisonment without legal help.

It is not difficult to imagine that, as a result of this system, there are considerable social, medical and legal problems which necessitate help from the South African Council of Churches. It is a pleasure to note that over 90 percent of the Council's budget is covered by contributions from churches in the Western world, while it is with anxiety we note that new laws are being prepared which will deprive the Council of the right to administer its own funds.

As already mentioned, racial discrimination is by no means limited to South Africa. Before the Second World War such discrimination was relatively common, and world opinion was not particularly concerned with it. The situation changed, however, after 1945: new ideas were expressed in the Atlantic Charter and the Declaration of Human Rights.

During the war it was possible to see signs of a more liberal policy evolving in South Africa. The ideas from the Atlantic Charter, however, had little effect there, and when the Nationalist Party won the election of 1948 the situation worsened. It was in this period that the apartheid laws were formulated and ratified, a move which has correctly been described as a counterrevolution against the pre-1948 tendencies.

History is never without a certain sense for the ironic—the man who more than anyone else was responsible for the implementation of the *apartheid* system, the Nationalist Party's first prime minister Dr. Daniel Malan, was a churchman, an ordained priest in the Dutch Reformed Church. And now we see that the most dynamic opponent of the *apartheid* system is also a churchman—in fact a bishop! In this way history corrects its own mistakes.

The irony of history is even more wide-ranging. The *apartheid* system is the indirect reason for the fact that Desmond Tutu became a churchman with the position he has today. His first wish was to become a doctor, but that was impossible with his parents' financial situation. He became, therefore, a teacher—as his father had been. In 1957 when the government introduced the state "Bantu education"—in many ways an abolition of education for the black population—Tutu felt himself driven from the teaching profession and began to study to be a priest. He has himself said that he did not feel himself called to take this step by high ideals, "it just occurred to me that, if the Church would have me, the profession of priest could be a good way of serving my people."

Yes—it seems that the Church was willing to take him!

Obviously, Desmond Tutu was not without high ideals. And, like so many others, he had those ideals from the family home. In his childhood in Klerksdorp in the West Rand district he was taught tolerance and sympathy. He has himself said that "I never learned to hate." The idealism of his parents was thus reflected in Tutu's upbringing.

When Tutu was twelve years old his family moved to Johannesburg, where his father was a teacher and his mother a cleaner and cook at a school for the blind. Here he learned sympathy for the weakest and most underprivileged. It was also here that he met the man who probably exercised the strongest influence over his formative years, the white priest Trevor Huddleston, who was parish priest in the black sum of Sophiatown. "One day," says Tutu, "I was standing in the street with my mother when a white man in a priest's clothing walked past. As he passed us he took off his hat to my mother. I couldn't believe my eyes—a white man who greeted a black working class woman!" When Tutu has in later years been asked why he doesn't hate whites, he usually replies that it is because he was fortunate in the white he met when young.

But, although he has never learnt to hate, no one has opposed injustice with a more burning anger. Courageous and fearless he opposed his country's authorities. He is to be found at the front of the demonstration processions, regardless of the danger to his own life. His clear standpoints and his fearless attitude have made him a unifying symbol for all groups of freedom campaigners in Africa.

Desmond Tutu has shown that to campaign for the cause of peace is not a question of silent acceptance, but rather of arousing consciences and a sense of indignation, strengthening the will and inspiring the human spirit so that it recognizes both its own value and its power of victory. To this fight for peace we give our affirmative "yes" today.

The actress Liv Ullman has told of a Lebanese boy who was asked if he believed in revenge. "Yes," replied the boy, he believed in revenge. "And to revenge," he was asked, "what is that?" "To revenge," replied the boy, "is to make a bad person a good person."

Thoughts of this nature are the human spirit's bulwark against barbarism. It is those who have such thoughts who are the real peacemakers and the meek, who are not only blessed, but who shall also inherit the earth—also the earth of South Africa. The 23 million colored people shall at least have the same right of inheritance to this as the 4.5 million whites.

The question has been raised whether the award of the Peace Prize to Desmond Tutu is to be seen as a judgment on the South African *apartheid* system. The answer is that the system has judged itself. Racial discrimination can never be anything but an expression of shameful contempt for humankind. Racial discrimination used and defended as a political system is totally incompatible with human civilization. This year's Peace Prize is therefore an attempt to awaken consciences. It is, and has to be, an illusion that privileged groups can maintain their position through repression. That such things can have a place in our future is a lie which nobody should allow themselves to believe.

In his famous book *Roots,* the black author Alex Haley tells of his African ancestor, the Negro slave Kunta Kinte, who attained the position of coachman with his white master. One of his duties was to drive his white masters to luxurious parties held at neighboring farms. One evening, as he sat outside and waited, he began to philosophize over his experiences. According to the author, he couldn't understand that such an unbelievable luxury really existed and that the whites really lived the way they did. After a long time and many such parties, he began to realize that the whites' existence was, in a remarkable way, unreal—a sort of beautiful dream built on a lie which the whites told themselves: that good can come of evil, and that it is possible to lead a civilized existence while not acknowledging as human beings those whose sweat and blood made their privileges possible.

Kunta Kinte was right. Negro slavery was incompatible with American civilization—in the same way as the *apartheid* system is in reality incompatible with South Africa.

There are few if any recorded examples in history of privileged groups who voluntarily relinquish privileges to the advantage of the repressed. In all probability it won't happen in South Africa either. The possibility of an unbloody resolution of the conflict is nevertheless still there. It is such a solution that Desmond Tutu fights for. The presentation of the Peace Prize to him is, therefore, not a judgment, rather it is a challenge, a hand stretched out—in the same way as Desmond Tutu's hand is stretched out to conciliation and atonement. If only the dominant minority would recognize this opportunity and take the chance before history's amnesty runs out.

It will be understood that to present Desmond Tutu's Nobel Peace Prize with a white man's hands is in some ways an oppressive experience. On such an occasion it is impossible not to allow one's thoughts to consider what the white man has perpetrated against his colored cousins. It is depressing to think of the list of debts which is written with the African's suffering, tears and blood. Think of the humiliation and exploitation which human beings from this continent have had to endure—from the first slave traffic, through centuries of colonialism and to today's discrimination. On a day like this our memories are indeed painful—not only on account of what the white man has done and still does, but also on account of what he, to this day, has neglected to do.

Thus, as we now present the Nobel Peace Prize to the African Desmond Tutu, our immediate feeling is that our first word to the Prize Laureate ought to be a word describing our sorrow over the wounds which injustice and racial hatred have inflicted on his people.

The dominating feeling is, however, one of thankfulness and respectful joy, and this is because we feel ourselves united with him in the belief in the creative power of love. With his warmhearted Christian faith he is a representative of the best in us all.

Additionally, there is a factor which the Nobel Committee has placed great emphasis on—that in the liberation process which Desmond Tutu leads, black and white stand shoulder to shoulder in the common cause against injustice. In this we see a moving confirmation of the words in Alfred Nobel's testament on the brotherhood of mankind.

In the light of this we bring our homage to Desmond Tutu. Because his struggle is—and has to be—our struggle, we recognize him as a brother. He receives today the Peace Prize as a sign of the thankfulness of millions—perhaps also as an omen of black and white Africans' final victory over the last remnants of opposition in the campaign for freedom and peace. It is appropriate to remember the words of Martin Luther King just before his martyrdom: "I have seen the Promised Land!"

Even though the black South African's way forward to freedom's promised land can still be long and difficult, it is a way of humanity which we shall traverse together in the sound knowledge that "we shall overcome." Therefore our first word to the Peace Prize laureate will be a word of hope and victory: "Oh yes, deep in my heart I do believe that we shall overcome—some day!" □

SPEECH OF ACCEPTANCE

ON BEING AWARDED THE NOBEL PEACE PRIZE

The Right Reverend Desmond Mpilo Tutu

Delivered on December 10, 1984, in Oslo Norway

Many thousands of people round the world have been thrilled with the award of the Nobel Peace Prize for 1984 to Desmond Mpilo Tutu. I was told of a delegation of American churchpeople who were visiting Russia. On hearing the news they and their Russian hosts celebrated the Nobel Peace Prize winner.

There has been a tremendous volume of greetings from heads of state, world leaders of the Christian church and other faiths as well as from so-called ordinary people—notable exceptions being the Soviet and South African governments.

The prize has given fresh hope to many in the world that has sometimes had a pall of despondency cast over it by the experience of suffering, disease, poverty, famine, hunger, oppression, injustice, evil and war—a pall that has made many wonder whether God cared, whether He was omnipotent, whether He was loving and compassionate. The world is in such desperate straits, in such a horrible mess that it all provides almost conclusive proof that a good and powerful and loving God such as Christians and people of other faiths say they believe in could not exist or if He did He really could not be a God who cared much about the fate of His creatures or the world they happened to inhabit which seemed to be so hostile to their aspirations to be fully human.

I once went to a friend's house in England.

There I found a charming book of cartoons entitled *My God*. One showed God with appeals and supplications bombarding Him from people below and He saying I wish I could say, "Don't call me, I'll call you." And another declared "Create in six days and have eternity to regret it." My favorite shows God somewhat disconsolate and saying, "Oh dear, I think I have lost my copy of the divine plan." Looking at the state of the world you would be forgiven for wondering if He ever had one and whether He had not really botched things up.

New hope has sprung in the breast of many as a result of this prize—the mother watching her mother starve in a bantustan homeland resettlement camp, or one whose flimsy plastic covering was demolished by the authorities in the K.T.C. squatter camp in Cape Town; the man emasculated by the pass laws as he lived for eleven months in a single-sex hostel, the student receiving an inferior education; the activist languishing in a consulate or a solitary confinement cell, being tortured because he thought he was human and wanted that God-given right recognized; the exile longing to kiss the soil of her much loved motherland, the political prisoner watching the days of a life sentence go by like the drip of a faulty tap, imprisoned because he knows she was created by God not to have his human dignity or pride trodden underfoot.

A new hope has been kindled in the breast of the millions who are voiceless, oppressed, dispossessed, tortured by the powerful tyrants; lacking elementary human rights in Latin America, in Southeast Asia, the Far East, in many parts of Africa and behind the Iron Curtain, who have their noses rubbed in the dust. How wonderful, how appropriate that this award is made today—December 10, Human Rights Day. It says more eloquently than anything else that this is God's world and He is in charge. That our cause is a just cause; that we will attain human rights in South Africa and everywhere in the world. We shall be free in South Africa and everywhere in the world.

I want to thank the Nobel Committee, I want to thank the Churches in Norway and everywhere for their support, their love and their prayers.

On behalf of all these for whom you have given new hope, a new cause for joy, I want to accept this award in a wholly representative capacity.

I accept this prestigious award on behalf of my family, on behalf of the South African Council of Churches, on behalf of all in my motherland, on behalf of those committed to the cause of justice, peace, and reconciliation everywhere.

If God be for us who can be against us? ☐

Eulogy

In Honor of Thurgood Marshall

Senator Carol Moseley Braun

Delivered in the United States Senate on January 26, 1993

Mr. President, Thurgood Marshall died last Sunday of heart failure. I still have great difficulty believing it. I know he was born over eighty-four years ago, and I know that he himself said he was "old and falling apart," but it is nonetheless hard to conceive that a heart as mighty and as courageous as his is no longer beating.

Thurgood Marshall epitomized the best in America; he was, in fact, what this country is all about. That may seem to be an odd thing to say about him. After all, he himself was very aware of the fact that the United States did not, and in too many instances still does not, live up entirely to its founding principles. He knew that the phrases of the Declaration of Independence, "that all men are created equal" and are endowed "with certain inalienable rights," including those to "life, liberty and the pursuit of happiness . . . ," were not, all too much of the time, the principles that govern everyday life in America.

Thurgood Marshall was born in Baltimore in 1908. He lived and felt the humiliation of racism, of not being able even to use the bathroom in downtown Baltimore simply because of the color of his skin.

But Thurgood Marshall was not defeated by racism. He knew that racial inequality was incompatible with American ideals, and he made it his life's unending fight to see that this country's ideals became true for all of its citizens.

And what a fight it has been. It took Thurgood Marshall from Baltimore's segregated public schools to Lincoln University, where he graduated with honors, to Howard University Law School, to the NAACP, to the circuit bench, to the U.S. Solicitor General's office, to become the first African-American member of the U.S. Supreme Court.

That quick biography does not begin to measure the battles Thurgood Marshall fought and won, and the strength, conviction and power he put into the fight.

Thomas Jefferson said that "A little rebellion, now and then, is a good thing, and as necessary in the political world as storms in the physical." Thurgood Marshall took Jefferson at his word, and played a key role in creating a rebellion in America, a rebellion not of violence, but of law. What Marshall did was to use the U.S. legal system to bludgeon and destroy state-supported segregation.

What Marshall did was to use the courts and the law to force the United States to apply the promises made every American in our Declaration of Independence and our Bill of Rights to African-Americans who had little or no protection under the law up until the Marshall legal rebellion. What Marshall did was to make the 13th, 14th, and 15th amendments to our Constitution the law of the land in reality, instead of just an empty promise.

The history of the civil rights movement in this country is, in no small part, the history of Marshall's battles before the Supreme Court. As lead counsel of the National Association for the Advancement of Colored People, Marshall appeared before the Supreme Court thirty-two times, and won twenty-nine times. His legal skills, grounded in sound preparation and sensitivity to the evidence, helped him win such landmark decisions as Smith versus Allwright, Shelley versus Kramer, Sweatt versus Painter, and the biggest case of them all, Brown versus Board of Education.

I am somewhat reluctant to dwell on Thurgood Marshall's many successes, because I know he would not like it. He would not like it because he knows only too well that there are many more battles that must be fought and won if America's founding principles and American reality are to become one and the same for every American of every color. In his dissent in the Bakke case, Marshall said:

> The position of the Negro today in America is the tragic but inevitable consequence of centuries of unequal treatment. Measured by any benchmark of comfort or achievement, meaningful equality remains a distant dream for the Negro.

However, the fact that the battle is not yet won does not lessen Marshall's many accomplishments. He was a man who worked and fought to make a difference; he was a man who did make a difference.

He certainly made a difference in my life, opening the doors of opportunity measured only by merit. He helped ensure that I was able to attend public schools and the University of Chicago Law School, and not schools for blacks only. His work helped make my election to the U.S. Senate possible. He opened closed doors and created new opportunities for me and for many, many others. His life was the most convincing evidence that change is possible.

I want to close, Mr. President, by quoting Thurgood Marshall one more time. In the Bakke case, he said:

> In light of the sorry history of discrimination and its devastating impact on the lives of Negroes, bringing the Negro into the mainstream of American life should be a state interest of the highest order.

I share his view. Elimination of racism is not just an interest of African-Americans, but of all Americans. Only then will we be able to tap the full potential of our people. Only then will we live the greatness of the American promise.

I hope we will all remember Thurgood Marshall by continuing his lifetime of struggle. I hope we will all remember Marshall by dedicating ourselves to the principles and goals he dedicated himself to: making American opportunity available to every American. And as we work toward those goals, I hope we can all live our lives as completely as he did, enjoy ourselves as much as he did, and poke as much fun at ourselves as Thurgood Marshall did all of his life.

I will miss Thurgood Marshall. America will miss Thurgood Marshall. I am proud to have the opportunity, in some small way, to continue his work, and to try to build on his legacy. □

TESTIMONIAL

JOE MORRISON
FRIEND AND COLLEAGUE

It has been said that "a thing of beauty is a joy forever," and while I would be the last person on earth to call Joe Morrison "beautiful," it does seem to be as if I have known him forever.

Joe, you and I go back quite a way, and we've had some good times, that's for certain. Yet, as I think back on the days, and sometimes the late nights, that we have worked together, I find it almost impossible to recall a time that wasn't "good." Of course, there were times we disagreed; times we agonized together over difficult decisions; times we were so besieged by work that there didn't seem time enough in the world to get it all done; times when budgets were defeated, enrollments were down, and we both wondered if it was too late to pursue some other career. Even so, looking back now with the perspective that only time can lend, all those occasions were "good times," mainly because you were there to share them.

Of course, I could speak of your intelligence; I could compliment your fantastic competence; I could point to you as a man of principles—a truly moral man whose honesty and integrity are unquestioned. Yes, I could do all of this, but all I would be doing is stating the obvious—obvious to anyone who has been blessed by knowing and working with you.

Instead, I'll just sum it up by saying that if I am proud of any single accomplishment in my life, it is this: Joe Morrison is my friend and colleague.

No one can deny that you have earned your retirement, and there is no one who is not delighted that you will finally be getting some time for yourself. At the same time, there is no one who does not realize that when you leave that administration building, there will occur a very real and palpable loss to this school district; that a part of what has made our school system the outstanding educational service that it is will have gone from us; that we will all somehow be the less for your absence.

We will miss you, Joe. We are thankful that you were here to contribute your thoughts and expertise to building our school system; we are honored that we have had the pleasure of being associated with you on a professional level; and we are overjoyed that we may call you our friend.

Godspeed, Joe. May your retirement be filled with the sparkling and golden days you so richly deserve. ☐

Keynote Speech

Ethics—A Global Business Challenge
Character and Courage

Robert D. Haas, Chairman of the Board and Chief Executive Officer, Levi Strauss & Co.

Delivered before the Conference Board, New York City, New York, May 4, 1994

We are meeting at a time when it seems that in every facet of contemporary life, people are placing self-interest ahead of ethical values. Pick up almost any day's edition of the *New York Times* and accounts of faltering ethical standards are chronicled in virtually every section of the paper. For purposes of my comments today, however, I want to focus on the business pages, since business and ethics is what we're here to talk about.

It wasn't so long ago that everyone had proclaimed that the "greed is good" spirit of the 1980s was dead and that the 1990s represented a return to basic values. But an honest evaluation of current business conduct contradicts that assessment, for example:

- Executives of American Honda are criminally indicted by Federal prosecutors for accepting bribes from dealers in exchange for franchises and hot-selling cars. Thirteen executives face potential prison terms that total 165 years behind bars.

- Corruption and mismanagement cause Gitano Jeans to lose its largest retail customer. The company's fortunes collapse. It's forced to file for bankruptcy and is ultimately sold.

- Prudential Securities is sued by its investors who allege it inappropriately sold limited partnerships. The scandal costs hundreds of millions of dollars, and the inquiry into possible corporate misdeeds extends in the company's most senior ranks.

- National Medical Enterprises agrees to pay more than $300 million to settle charges of health insurance fraud and patient abuse.

It should hardly come as a surprise that such incidents have led to an erosion of public confidence and an eruption of distrust in the major institutions of our society—including business.

But these accounts of ethical misconduct are not unique to the U.S.—as recent scandals in Great Britain, Japan, Brazil, Russia and elsewhere suggest. In my comments today, however, I intend to talk primarily about what's going on here in America.

While price fixing conspiracies, bribery, fraud and business collusion are not the norm of contemporary business practice, they occur far more frequently that we care to acknowledge—and clearly more often than is permissible to gain the level of public trust and support that business requires to thrive.

What is most puzzling about instances of business wrongdoing is that they clearly contradict both the values that are held by most of us as individuals and the collective stands that we have established for appropriate business behavior.

When pressed about his company's payment of bribes to Italian political parties in the '80s, the chairman of Olivetti made the startling confession that he personally authorized the payment of bribes and added that he would do it again to protect his company's interest.

In his famous essay on civil disobedience, Henry David Thoreau wrote that a corporation

> has not conscience, but a corporation of conscientious men is a corporation with a conscience.

I'd like to think that if Thoreau were writing today he would have spoken of both men *and women* with a conscience, though regrettably the corporate world remains more of a male enclave than it should be.

If Thoreau is correct, and I believe he is, how do we help honorable men and women confront and address the ethical challenges they face in the everyday world of work? This is the puzzle all of us must work to solve.

In my remarks this morning, I'd like to talk about some of the ethical struggles that we've faced at my own company and how we've dealt with them.

I'd like to begin by conducting a brief quiz. By the way, these are the same questions I raise with my associates at Levi Strauss & Co. when I lead one of our ethics training programs.

As I ask these five questions, please respond by raising your hands.

- First, how many of you consider yourselves to be ethical people?

- How many of you believe that it's important for business to function in an ethical manner?

- How many of you believe that you know an ethical dilemma when you see it?

- How many of you feel there are clear answers to ethical problems?

- Now, how many of you believe that I always know an ethical dilemma when it arises and always know how to resolve it?

Clearly, all of us feel strongly about ethics in the abstract. But at the same time, each of us is keenly aware of the struggle we face as ethical dilemmas arise. It is this common struggle—between our own desire to be ethical and the competing pressures of business performance—that brings us here today.

I should admit that when I approached the microphone this morning, I did so with some trepidation because of this very fact. While I am honored to be able to keynote this important, two-day conference, like everyone in this room, we at Levi Strauss & Co. struggle every day with how to create a business culture that promotes ethical behavior.

All of us can cite our own experiences about ethical problems we've encountered or witnessed first-hand. The real value of this conference is that each of us can offer our own ideas about how to help managers and employees apply their own high ethical standards in the workplace, so that they don't have to check their values at the door when they show up for work. Over the next two days, I know you will reap the mutual benefit of your collective ideas and experiences.

As part of this conference, I understand you'll be examining the ethics programs of a number of companies. As you go through this exercise, you might find it useful to bear in mind the three very different approaches to dealing with ethical dilemmas that characterize how companies approach these ethics.

These are:

1. Neglect—or the absence of any formal ethical programs;
2. Compliance-based programs; and,
3. Values-oriented programs.

I'd like to spend a few moments touching on each of these three concepts.

It's hard to imagine that any large company could rationally ignore the importance of ethics or fail to develop management policies and programs given the effect ethical breaches can have on financial performance, sales and corporate reputation. But some companies clearly don't get the message.

According to the Institute for Crisis Management, more than one-half of the news crisis stories filed in 1993 were crises brought on by the questionable judgment of management—firings, white-collar crime, government investigations and discrimination suits. Coverage of these types of corporate misdeeds has risen 55 percent since 1989, while coverage of "operational" crises—chemical spills, product tamperings—has declined 4 percent.

Obviously, there are grave consequences for ignoring ethical problems. There is also increasing evidence from academic studies that show positive correlations between responsible business behavior and return-on-investment, stock price, consumer preferences and employee loyalty.

The companies that ignore ethics do so based on assumptions that are false and never challenged. They seem to view ethics either as unimportant or as a costly and inconvenient luxury.

I think they're wrong on both accounts.

I believe—and our company's experience demonstrates—that a company cannot sustain success unless it develops ways to anticipate and address ethical issues as they arise. Doing the right thing from day one helps avoid future setbacks and regrets. Addressing ethical dilemmas when they arise may save your business from serious financial or reputational harm.

Many companies share this view, and a number of them have chosen a second approach to ethics—what Lynn Sharp Paine, an associate professor at Harvard, refers to as compliance-based programs. These ethics programs are most often designed by corporate counsel. They are based on rules and regulations, with the goal of preventing, detecting, and publishing legal violations.

Until recently, we were among the companies that took this approach. The centerpiece of our efforts was a comprehensive collection of regulations that spelled out our worldwide code of business ethics. In it, we laid out rules for hiring practices, travel and entertainment expenses, political contributions, compliance with local laws, improper payments, gifts and favors. We addressed topics ranging from accounting practices to potential conflicts of interest. As you might guess, it was a long and weighty list of do's and don'ts for our people to follow.

This approach didn't serve us well. First, rules beget rules. And regulations beget regulations. We became buried in paperwork, and any time we faced a unique ethical issue, another rule or regulation was born. Second, our compliance-based program sent a disturbing message to our people—WE DON'T RESPECT YOUR INTELLIGENCE OR TRUST YOU! Finally, and one of the most compelling reasons for shedding this approach, was that it didn't keep managers or employees from exercising poor judgment and making questionable decisions.

We learned that you can't force ethical conduct into an organization. Ethics is a function of the collective attitudes of our people. And these attitudes are cultivated and supported by at least seven factors:

1. commitment to responsible business conduct;
2. management's leadership;
3. trust in employees;
4. programs and policies that provide people with clarity about the organization's ethical expectations;
5. open, honest and timely communications;
6. tools to help employees resolve ethical problems; and
7. reward and recognition systems that reinforce the importance of ethics.

Ultimately, high ethical standards can be maintained only if they are modeled by management and woven into the fabric of the company. Knowing this, your challenge and mine is to cultivate the kind of environment where people do the right thing.

Realizing the importance of each of these elements led Levi Strauss & Co.— and a growing number of other companies—to try a third approach to ethics, based on a values-orientation. This method combines functional values with individual responsibility and accountability.

Today, at Levi Strauss & Co., we base our approach to ethics upon six ethical principles—honesty, promise-keeping, fairness, respect for others, compassion and integrity.

Using this approach, we address ethical issues by first identifying which of these ethical principles applies to the particular business decision. Then, we determine which internal and which external stakeholders' ethical concerns should influence our business decisions. Information on stakeholder issues is gathered and possible recommendations are discussed with "high influence" stakeholder groups, such as shareholders, employees, customers, members of local communities, public interest groups, our business partners, and so forth.

This principle-based approach balances the ethical concerns of these various stakeholders with the values of our organization. It is a process that extends trust to an individual's knowledge of the situation. It examines the complexity of issues that must be considered in each decision, and it defines the role each person's judgment plays in carrying out his or her responsibilities in an ethical manner.

We're integrating ethics with our other corporate values, which include diversity, open communications, empowerment, recognition, teamwork and honesty, into every aspect of our business—from our human resource practices to our relationships with our business partners.

I'd like to illustrate how we're linking ethics and business conduct with an area of increasing importance to many global corporations—the contract manufacturing of products in developing countries.

Because Levi Strauss & Co. operates in many countries and diverse cultures, we take special care in selecting contractors in those countries where our goods are produced. We do this to ensure that our products are being made in a manner consistent with our values and that protects our brand image and corporate reputation. So, in 1991, we developed a set of Global Sourcing Guidelines.

Our guidelines describe the business conduct we require of our contractors. For instance, the guidelines ban the use of child or prison labor. They stipulate certain environmental requirements. They limit working hours and mandate regularly scheduled days off. Workers must have the right of free association and not be exploited. At a minimum, wages must comply with the law and match prevailing local practice and working conditions must be safe and healthy. We also expect our business partners to be law abiding and to conduct all of their business affairs in an ethical way.

In developing our guidelines, we also recognized that there are certain issues beyond the control of our contractors, so we produced a list of "country selection" criteria. For example, we will not source in countries where conditions, such as the human rights climate, would run counter to our values and have an adverse effect on our global brand image or damage our corporate reputation.

Similarly, we will not source in countries where circumstances threaten our employees while traveling, where the legal climate makes it difficult or jeopardizes our trademarks, and where political or social turmoil threatens our commercial interest.

Since adopting our guidelines, we've terminated our business relationships with about 5 percent of our contractors and required workplace improvements of another 25 percent. Likewise, we announced a phased withdrawal from contracting in China and exited Burma due to human rights concerns, although we remain hopeful that the human rights climate in these countries will improve so we can alter these decisions.

In the process of creating our guidelines, we formed a working group of fifteen employees from a broad cross-section of the company. The working group spent nine months formulating our guidelines. In crafting these guidelines, they used our principle-based decision-making model to guide their deliberations.

Drafting these guidelines was difficult. Applying them has proven even more challenging.

When we were rolling out our guidelines—which included extensive on-site audits of each of our seven hundred contractors worldwide—we discovered that two of our manufacturing contractors in Bangladesh and one in Turkey employed under-age workers. This was a clear violation of our guidelines, which prohibit the use of child labor. At the outset, it appeared that we had options:

- Instruct our contractors to fire these children, knowing that many are the sole wage earners for their families and that if they lost their jobs, their families would face extreme hardships.

or we could:

- Continue to employ under-age children, ignoring our stance against the use of child labor.

By referencing our ethical guidelines to decision making we came up with a different approach and one that we believe helped to minimize adverse ethical consequences.

The contractors agreed to pay the under-age children their salaries and benefits while they go to school full-time. We agreed to pay for books, tuition and uniforms. When the children reach legal working age, they will be offered jobs in the plant. Due to these efforts, thirty-five children have attended school in Bangladesh, while another six are currently in school in Turkey.

And how did we benefit from this situation?

We were able to retain quality contractors that play an important role in our worldwide sourcing strategy. At the same time, we were able to honor our values and protect our brands.

Applying our sourcing guidelines has forced us to find creative solutions to vexing ethical dilemmas. Clearly, at times, adhering to these standards has added costs. To continue working for us, some contractors have added emergency exits and staircases, increased ventilation, reduced crowding, improved bathroom facilities and invested in water-treatment systems. The costs of these requirements have been passed on to us—at least in part—in the form of higher product prices. In other cases, we have foregone less expensive sources of production due to unsatisfactory working conditions or concerns about the country of origin.

Conventional wisdom holds that these added costs put us at a competitive disadvantage. Yes, they limit our options somewhat and squeeze profit margins in the near-term. But over the years, we've found that decisions which emphasize cost to the exclusion of all other factors don't serve a company's and its shareholders' long-term interests.

Moreover, as a company that invests hundreds of millions of advertising dollars each year to create consumer preference for our products, we have a huge stake in protecting that investment. In today's world, a television exposé on working conditions can undo years of effort to build brand loyalty. Why squander your investment when, with foresight and commitment, reputational problems can be prevented?

But you don't have to take my word for it.

There is a growing body of evidence that shows a positive correlation between good corporate citizenship and financial performance. Studies by leading research groups such as Opinion Research Corporation and Yankelovich Partners, respected scholars and socially responsible investment firms, underscore the point that companies which look beyond solely maximizing wealth and profits and are driven by values and a sense of purpose outperform those companies that focus only on short-term gain.

Companies with strong corporate reputations have been shown to outperform the S&P 500, have higher sales, sustain greater profits and have stocks that outperform the market. These are results that no bottom-line-fixated manager can ignore.

Similarly, a recent study suggests that how a company conducts itself affects consumer purchasing decisions and customer loyalty. A vast majority—84 percent—of the American public agrees that a company's reputation can well be the deciding factor in terms of what product or service they buy.

These findings mirror our own experience. Our values-driven approach has helped us:

- identify contractors who want to work for Levi Strauss & Co. to achieve our "blue ribbon" certification, enhancing their own business stature;

- we have gained retailer and consumer loyalty. Retailers feel good about having us as business partners because of our commitment to ethical practices. Today's consumer has more products to chose from and more information about those products. A company's reputation forms a part of the consumers' perceptions of the product and influences purchasing decisions.

At the same time:

- we're better able to attract, retain and motivate the most talented employees, because the company's values more closely mirror their own personal values.

- because government and community leaders view us as a responsible corporate citizen we have been welcomed to do business in established and emerging markets.

Let me conclude with a few last thoughts.

We are living in an environment in which ethical standards and behaviors are being increasingly challenged. Addressing these dilemmas becomes even more difficult when you overlay the complexities of different cultures and values systems that exist throughout the world. For example, in some cultures honesty will take precedence over caring—"tell the truth even if it hurts"; whereas other cultures find caring or "saving face" as the predominant value.

As you grapple with some fictitious ethical quandaries over the next two days, I encourage you to ask yourself these questions:

- "How much am I willing to compromise my principles?"
- "Are there times when I'm willing to risk something I value for doing the right thing?"

For me and my associates at Levi Strauss & Co. I think the answers have become clear: Ethics must trump all other considerations. Ultimately, there are important commercial benefits to be gained from managing your business in a responsible and ethical way that best serves your enterprises' long-term interests. The opposite seems equally clear: the dangers of not doing so are profound.

Michael Josephson, a noted ethics expert, defined ethics this way:

> Ethics is about character and courage and how we meet the challenge when doing the right thing will cost more than we want to pay.

The good news is that courage carries with it a great reward—the prospect of sustained responsible commercial success. I think that's what each of us wants our legacy to be. And I believe ultimately our key stakeholders—all of them—will accept nothing less. ☐

DEDICATION SPEECH

LADY LIBERTY

Lee A. Iacocca

Delivered at the "Year of Liberty" concert in Washington, D.C., on October 28, 1985

Good evening to all of you.

I've been privileged for the past three and a half years to be involved in restoring two of our nation's most valuable treasures—the Statue of Liberty and Ellis Island. And it's been a labor of love, believe me.

A year from today, the Lady with the Torch will be rededicated on her hundredth birthday, and tonight we begin the celebration of her centennial year.

All this is possible because millions of Americans have contributed more than $170 million so far to keep the torch lit. You've been invited tonight so we could thank you for your generous support.

And we're going to thank you with the world premiere of Richard Adler's "The Lady Remembers" performed by the Detroit Symphony Orchestra, under the direction of Gunther Herbig, with soloist Julia Migenes Johnson.

You know, the last couple of years lots of school kids have been sending me their nickels and dimes for the Lady. Some even send me their lunch money, or a few bucks from selling cupcakes or washing cars. And a man once dropped into my office and gave me a million dollars to help shine her up. (As he said "just a simple tribute to my immigrant mother.") It seems like everybody feels they owe the Lady something.

And Richard Adler is one of those people.

Richard Adler wasn't *commissioned* to write this piece. He wasn't *asked* to do it. He simply called one day and said: "I *want* to do it. I *need* to do it. Just *let* me do it."

So we let him do it.

It's quite a gift he's giving us, and giving America, tonight. So, please join me in expressing our thanks to Richard Adler.

And now we are about to honor a very, very special lady.

She's a lady who has stood tall and strong at the doorstep of our country for nearly a hundred years. She has stood with a beacon raised to guide the lost . . . with an arm outstretched to welcome the homeless . . . and with a tablet proclaiming her promise of liberty.

We not only honor that lady tonight, but also the millions who saw her beacon and reached out for her welcome . . . because they believed her promise.

And we honor what *they* did to keep her promise alive, and to pass it along to all of us.

Exactly ninety-nine years ago today, a beautiful lady dressed in two hundred tons of copper and iron stood staring through the mist in New York Harbor, a little like a blushing bride. Quite a fuss was made over her that day. Cannons roared, brass bands played, all the ships in the harbor blew their whistles and rang their bells.

She was that day a young symbol of an old but elusive dream—the simple ideal of liberty. Tonight, ninety-nine years later but forever young, she stands not only for that original ideal itself, but also as a symbol of what free people, guided and protected by that ideal, can achieve.

For as soon as the cannons and the bands were silent, she began to see the ships slipping into the harbor with the first of the millions of immigrants she would welcome to America.

Tonight she remembers those ships coming from Bremen and Liverpool and Naples . . . and the cargo they brought. Human beings seeking refuge and opportunity beneath her torch.

They all stood on deck in their best clothes . . . clutching the kids, and maybe an old cardboard suitcase with a rope around it. It was the biggest day of their lives.

And as the ships went by her on their way to Ellis Island, a lot of backs, bent by oppression, began to straighten. And a lot of faces, scarred by tyranny, were suddenly smiling. And a lot of eyes, dimmed by despair, began to glow with hope.

She saw all that, and she remembers it well tonight.

She remembers, too, what happened to them after they passed beyond her gaze.

She *kept* her promise of liberty, but it wasn't the liberty of streets paved with gold. It was the liberty of the shovel, the freedom of the pushcart, and the dignity of the plow.

It was the freedom to work hard, and to keep what that hard work built.

They were ambitious in a time when *ambition* was not a dirty word.

They were hardworking in a time when hard work was not something to be avoided.

They were builders.

They built a country.

And what they built was the America we have today—imperfect, but better by far than anything anybody else has ever built, anywhere.

The Lady remembers how they did it, and so should we.

They did it with pain, and sweat and tears.

You know, America isn't great because of its natural resources. It's great because those people dug into the ground, often under terrible conditions, and took the resources out.

America isn't great because of miles of open prairies. It's great because people broke their backs to bust the sod and grow food.

America isn't great because of a few industrial geniuses. It's great because of the thousands of others who fired the furnaces and forged the metal.

And America isn't great because of a piece of paper called a Constitution. It's great because people fought, and bled, and sometimes died to fulfill its promise of a just and humane society.

So, the Lady remembers, if sometimes we forget. She remembers who we are and where we came from.

We're all her children . . . whether she saw our people arrive on those ships from Europe . . . or whether they came on the Mayflower . . . or from Africa in chains . . . or from the Far East or Latin America.

She is a special lady to all of us, and we honor her tonight . . . because she remembers, and because she helps all of us remember . . . just what kind of people we are.

Thank you. ☐

PUBLIC RELATIONS SPEECH

2001: A RETAILING ODYSSEY
CONFRONTING THE CONSUMER OF THE 21ST CENTURY

Wendy Liebmann, President, WSL Marketing, Inc.

Delivered before a Meeting of Retail Executives Sponsored by Clairol, Scottsdale, Arizona, January 27, 1995

I was asked to speak to you today about consumer trends. That's sometimes a dangerous pursuit because the speed at which things change in this country and around the world is so great that before you know it today's trend is yesterday's memory.

This cartoon from *Advertising Age* sums it up perfectly. For those of you who can't see it . . . that's a trend we'll discuss later . . . there's a man sitting at his desk (another trend we'll talk about later) listening to his voice mail (yet another trend we'll talk about later) and the message is, "while you were away from your desk the following trends have bitten the dust."

Talking about trends is a rather precarious pursuit, especially when one makes predictions about the future to "captains of industry," such as yourselves (that's a trend we'll talk about later) especially to captains of industry who have good memories.

But having never been fainthearted I'm willing to jump right in.

Let's begin by agreeing to an important fact—not a trend. A reality. If you think today is January 27, 1995, you are sadly mistaken. Today is actually January 27, 2001, and your odyssey has begun. So let's all say "good morning Hal" and get on with it.

Let's use the *Ad Age* cartoon as a reference point, remembering that it's 2001 and let's talk about consumers—your customers—who they are, how they live, what they want and how you can satisfy them when you get back to your office next Monday, January 30, 2001.

What's wrong with this picture? There is a man in it. Now I am not suggesting that today, in 2001, men are no longer a factor in the work force, but I am suggesting their importance and role will have changed. That's *trend number one.*

Consider this: in 1988, 15 percent of preschool children were cared for by their fathers while their mothers worked. In 1991, the number increased to 20 percent. Today in 2001, nearly one in three preschool children are cared for by their fathers.

Why? First, the percentage of women in the labor force is growing, while the percentage of men is declining. In 1980, 48 percent of the labor force were women sixteen years and older. In 1990, 55 percent were women. And according to the census bureau, today in 2001, women are 62 percent of the labor force.

Second, in 2001, 33 percent of corporate relocations involve women employees, up from 18 percent in 1992; of trailing spouses, 25 percent are men in 2001, up from 15 percent in 1990.

Third, in 2001, more than 40 percent of small businesses are owned by women, up from 32 percent in 1990.

So what does that mean? It means more and more that the "captains" of industry are now women. As a result, they are no longer the primary caregivers, nor the primary shoppers in the family because they are too busy—out earning the family living.

That means more and more often, men are doing the family shopping and taking care of the home.

That means more and more often, men are buying the groceries, toiletries, prescriptions, home furnishings, even clothing for the kids.

No longer is their shopping confined to Home Depot, Circuit City or the local car dealership. They are at the supermarket, drugstore, discounter and anywhere else their household shopping list takes them.

They are doing the cooking, the cleaning, taking the kids to school, to the barber and the doctor. No longer is their involvement in the home confined to programming the new VCR or taking out the garbage.

That means successful marketers and retailers of the 21st century must focus their attention on making the shopping environment easy for both men and women.

That's not so simple since men and women shop differently. Men spend less time shopping. They browse less. They spend more money. They are more brand loyal.

Then of course, there's the difference in the level of shopping experience. Women have had years at it. Not so men. Smart companies will help men find their way through the experience.

Imagine this: you are in aisle four—the toiletries aisle—of one of your stores, and for the very first time you are confronted by 15 feet of shampoo. Is that a daunting experience—or what?

Add to that picture a two-year-old child tugging at your hand. She needs to go to the bathroom. Now choose the right shampoo for the first time. The same holds true for cough medicine, diapers, vitamins, hair colorant, you get the picture.

Brand names, product information, sales assistance, a place to keep little Timmy or Mary occupied while dad shops, will make the shopping experience less overwhelming, and make dad more loyal to your store.

Keep this in mind, if one of every three people coming through your door shopping for the family in 2001 is a man, like you, how can you make it easier for him? Guess what? If you make it easier for him, believe me you will make it easier for your women shoppers too.

What else is wrong with this picture? This man is white, of Anglo-American extraction, which brings us to *trend number two:* the impact of changing ethnic diversity of the country. By 2001, nearly 30 percent of the population will be non-Anglo. Eleven percent are Hispanic, 12 percent African American, 4 percent Asian.

I know you've heard all of this before. I know in the 1990s, many of you made adjustments in your business to accommodate the changing diversity in this country.

I'm sure, without exception, you all adjusted your product mixes in those markets that you defined as ethnically diverse, adding ethnic brands, colors, dual-language product information, ethnic store employees, and so on.

But that's just the beginning. The differences are much more subtle and significant. Did you know that Asian and Hispanic Americans spend more money on groceries per week than the average American family? They did in 1994. While the average American household spent $65 a week on groceries, Asian-American households spent $87 and Hispanic households $91.

Part of the reason was that Asian and Hispanic households were larger. However, just as significant—if not more so—was the fact that these ethnic groups were—and are—much more likely to buy branded products and spend more money for quality.

Nationally advertised brands mean quality to these Americans. And they are much more likely to choose quality over price. What does that say for your product mix? What are the implications for your private label business?

And this was just the beginning. Both in our WSL Marketing "How America Shops" consumer studies and in other market segmentation research, it has become very clear that marketing to the increasingly diverse American marketplace means much more than offering sales and hair straightening products.

Did you know, for example, based on a 1994 study, that while 46 percent of Anglo Americans purchased diet soft drinks in a month, other ethnic groups purchased them much less frequently: 30 percent of Hispanics, 25 percent of African Americans and only 17 percent of Asian Americans?

You might think this has a whole lot to do with different attitudes toward diet and weight and to some degree that is true. However, a major factor is not low calorie-related at all. It is, in fact, the result of a different attitude some ethnic groups have to drinking carbonated soft drinks in general.

For example, in the same study, while seven out of ten Anglo Americans and Hispanic Americans purchased regular carbonated soft drinks in a month, only 55 percent of African Americans and 48 percent of Asian Americans followed suit. So now you know why the 99 cent soda specials don't work as effectively in all your markets.

Soda aside: how about analgesics? Did you know that while one-in-three Americans purchased an analgesic each month, nearly 60 percent of Hispanic Americans did?

Did you know that Anglo Americans spend significantly less on clothing per month than other ethnic groups, in particular Hispanic and African-American families? (What an opportunity for discounters.) Did you know that non-Anglo Americans use fewer coupons?

What does all this mean for you in 2001? It means that the differences in purchasing behavior of different ethnic groups are not as obvious and clear cut as you might think.

And as we move into the 21st century, your sensitivity to these differences and your flexibility and adaptability will mean the difference between success and failure.

What else is wrong with the cartoon? This man is wearing glasses.

When I first put up the cartoon I suggested there were a number of things wrong with it. Some of you may not be able to see it . . . at least without your glasses. Don't worry about it because it's 2001 and you don't need glasses any more. Laser surgery corrected your eyesight. A brief operation in the doctor's office, easier than filling a tooth used to be in the 20th century. Now you have 20:20 vision.

Not only can you see perfectly but you have thrown out all those glasses you used to lose. Wonder why sales of magnifying glasses are declining so rapidly in the 21st century?

Which brings us to *trend number three:* the "middle aging" of Americans. In 2001 27 percent of Americans are over fifty. They have refused to accept the inconveniences of middle age. Because of their significant numbers and clout, medical technology has addressed their needs.

While at the moment it has only gone as far as correcting eyesight, within the next decade medical science will have developed quick, easy and permanent ways to replace arthritic joints, correct hearing loss and incontinence and many other physical conditions of age.

Consider what that means. Remember the magnifying glasses? Now think about the decline in sales of analgesics, hearing aid batteries and incontinence products.

And you thought an aging population would mean increased sales of "old people's" products. As a wise old Australian once said, "Nothing lasts forever, dearie." In this day and age, forever is a very short time.

But the good news in all this is, that in spite of the decline in some categories, it also means people, consumers, we, are around longer, and in better shape to go shopping. So there you have trend number three.

What else is wrong with this picture? This man is wearing a suit and tie. Way before 2001, America was a "casual" society, with jeans and sneakers the preferred attire—at least on our own time.

But as we moved through the stress-filled, economically distracted early '90s, many companies offered their employees the "chill out" option of wearing casual clothes to work—at least on Fridays. That's *trend number four.*

By 2001, casual work attire has become an everyday option. In fact, in 1994 it was fast moving in that direction, with 31 percent of office workers usually wearing casual attire to work, and 90 percent sometimes doing so. With the comfort and ease casual attire brings, your employees will be more productive and creative. That's the good news.

But productivity and creativity aside, why should you care? Well, first there are your sales of panty hose. (Wonder why they have declined of late? Now you know.) But after that?

Since you are not in the apparel business you don't have to try to compete, as department stores now do, with lower priced, more casual clothing outlets such as the Gap, Penneys, Sears, Wal-Mart, Kmart, Target . . . well, of course you do.

As more and more consumers have reason to buy casual clothes, they shop in those outlets that sell casual clothes at everyday low prices. Yes—the discount stores. And while there, they will be more inclined to buy their toiletries, prescriptions, cosmetics, film, greeting cards and diapers.

But it's not all that bad. If consumers shop less in department stores for clothes, they will also buy fewer beauty products there. So there's a chance to compensate for the panty hose.

Speaking of beauty products, *trend number five*. This man has gray hair. In 2001 this is not so. In 1994, sales of men's hair coloring products grew 20 percent—even faster than women's products (women's products grew 17.5 percent). In 2001, hair coloring products for men is one of the fastest growing personal care categories.

Remember the "middle-aging of Americans" discussion? This is where you make up for the lost sales of reading glasses. Because as we all get older, we will color our hair—all of us—more and more. Men will be the biggest users, especially as they feel the need to stay younger-looking to compete in the work force longer.

But not just hair color. Skin care in particular will be a major category for men. Do you remember how we used to talk about the future of the men's beauty market? And how, year after year, people would predict "the future is nigh"? And yet it didn't happen.

Sure, there were increases in sales of shaving products and fragrance. But that, for years, was that. Well, that is no longer that. Today in 2001, the male grooming market is $12 billion—double the size it was in 1993.

We finally discovered the missing link. And it is age. So just as women who get older use more skin care and hair care products, so too will you.

In fact, I suspect if we go around the room and ask what personal care products (I wouldn't dare call them beauty products) you use regularly, there will be a whole lot of you who now use a facial moisturizer, after shave, fragrance, lip balm, maybe even a self-tanner.

But let's be clear. Selling beauty products to men in 2001 requires finesse. For just as you may not feel comfortable discussing in public what you use, nor will your customers. Education, assistance and information will be the keys. The influx of men's magazines such as *Men's Health* and *Men's Journal* will educate your customers, but you'll have to make them feel at ease walking your aisles. That's trend number five.

What else is wrong with this picture? This man is working in an office outside his home. Not in 2001.

Trend number six—there are a growing number of people working in their homes—those who are self-employed and those employed by corporations.

It began in the '80s as people lost their jobs and set up their own businesses. It began as women juggled jobs and families. It evolved as large corporations "outsourced" some of their functions to be more cost-effective; as people moved further and further away from their jobs in an effort to find affordable housing. And it continued as companies realized it was more essential for their employees to be productive than it was for them to come to an office every day.

So what does that mean in 2001? Well, aside from the fact that you can probably get rid of your corporate headquarters—just a joke—it means that products and services suited for the home office will boom, whether it's computers, furniture, stationery, electronics or convenience food. (We still have to eat—and we want something that's easy, single serving, healthy, to whip in the microwave at lunchtime.)

Outlets that sell these categories conveniently, inexpensively and with service will boom. After all that what happens if my modem goes on the fritz just as I'm about to send a report to my boss?

Which leads me to *trend number seven*. The over-publicized, under-comprehended, will-it-ever-happen, and in-what-form information highway. Well in 2001 it is here. And no Virginia, it is not based on five hundred cable channels.

It is based on the PC, with modem, fax, telephone, on-line services, CD-ROM, all connected to your U.S. corporate headquarters in Miami, your international headquarters in Beijing, your winter home in Missoula, and your summer home in Bora Bora. Think I'm kidding? The only kidding part is where you will live.

You will "speak" not type reports, hold meetings with management on three continents, "walk" the real estate for a new warehouse facility, review a sales problem with your manager in store 103, check your stock price, book airline tickets, order a new suit, shop for a Valentine's gift, check out a new car, and watch a movie without budging from your home office in Missoula, or Bora Bora.

Think I'm crazy? In 1994 you could perform every one of these functions from your computer if you wanted to. Did you?

Want to check out a new car? How about the new Toyota Avalon? Take a look at this. Available on a free computer disk, with motion and sound. As simple as clicking on the icon to see the car from every angle, with all its features, price and all. And, no annoying car salesmen until you're ready to test drive. Thought I was crazy?

Which leads to *trend number eight*. If I can do all that on a computer, why should I ever go into a store to shop?

After all, on a good day in the '90s, shopping for most of us was a chore. The days of going shopping for fun had long gone. It was all a matter of necessity. All we prayed for was that we could find a parking spot, get in, get what we wanted and get out as quickly and inexpensively as possible.

To avoid stores in the '90s a whole lot of us spent $60+ billion through catalogs, on TV and on-line. Even then we could buy everything from prescriptions to eye glasses, clothes, food, beauty products, health products, hosiery, electronics and just about anything else we needed.

But thanks to the technological changes we've seen since the end of the '90s, shopping in 2001 has become a pleasure again.

First because the day-to-day repetitive stuff—you know, milk, orange juice, soda, butter, toilet tissue, shampoo, mascara, socks, underwear—is all done from the comfort of your chair at home, sitting in front of the computer.

Open the screen, highlight the store name, enter your store debit card number and begin. Pick your category, scroll down the menu, pick your brand, check the price, select the quantity, aisle by aisle, category by category, until you finish your shopping list and enter how and when you want the merchandise delivered.

Think it won't happen? Think again. Consumers have no time. We didn't have any in 1994 and we certainly don't have any now. Remember what I said at the beginning. More women working, more men juggling house duties. Shopping for basics is not fun. It's a necessity. If I don't have to go to the store to do it— why do it?

Even in the '90s, there were growing opportunities to shop for basics—replenishment shopping—without going into the store. I'm not talking about catalog shopping or TV shopping but shopping for everyday basic commodities.

Stores offered programs where you could reorder your panty hose to be automatically shipped to you every month. No fuss. At Bloomingdales you could order your cosmetics via phone or fax. You could reorder your contact lenses or prescriptions without going to the store.

At select Safeway or Eckerd stores you could place your grocery order or buy drug store products on-line via computer. And that was in 1994.

Maybe you think it won't happen because your customers don't know how to use a computer, are not comfortable doing so, or don't have one at home. Well, think again, because even in 1994 one out of every three homes in America had a personal computer. The number was even higher for households with children— over 40 percent.

In the end, that's the key. Not our generation, but our kids and our grandchildren. They cut their teeth on computers. Anyone under thirty has. As television was the technological breakthrough for our generation, the computer was for theirs. And they are your future customers. They're the ones you need to start thinking about in the 21st century.

But you will be relieved to know that, in spite of all the technological changes, retail stores as we knew them in the '90s have not disappeared in the 21st century. But they certainly have changed.

What has happened is that shopping outside the home—what I call "four walls" shopping—is no longer the utilitarian, often exhausting and frequently frustrating experience it used to be in the '90s. Because shopping—store shopping—in the 21st century is all about entertainment and fun.

Remember entertainment? Remember when we used to talk about "department stores as theater"? Remember when new store openings meant pony rides in the parking lot and free watermelon?

Remember when cosmeticians used to do makeovers in all you stores? Remember when you were invited to your local department store—no, not for a sale—but to see a fashion show of the latest season's clothes? Remember when going shopping was an event? Meet your friends, have lunch, pick up a date. Have fun?

Well, that fast disappeared in the '80s and early '90s as more and more retailers, starved for profits, eliminated services, reduced creative promotions, cut back on any vestiges of excitement and drove business by those nefarious "sale" signs, coupons and 99 cent specials.

Never slow to respond, and never ever stupid, consumers no longer saw any advantage to paying more, so went shopping at the lowest-priced outlet in town.

Well, it's 2001, and shopping and entertainment have become intertwined once again. The rebirth began in the '90s. Remember the Mall of America with its Knotts Berry Farm, gigantic Snoopy and roller coaster rides? Remember the Disney and Warner Brothers stores with multimedia, larger than life Daffy Duck running amok and Superman flying from the ceiling? With Bugs Bunny videos, dolls, jackets, mugs and ties. And there's no forgetting the Nike store with half court all ready for that quick game of one-on-one before you bought your latest sneakers.

Remember Barnes & Noble bookstores where the experience and pure joy of reading enveloped you? With comfortable armchairs to plonk down in and read undisturbed, and an in-store coffee bar to re-fortify you. Or Williams-Sonoma with cooking demonstrations and free, fresh-baked cookies. Ah, the smell of it. That was just the beginning.

Those retailers who are succeeding in the 21st century understand that retailing is no longer just a function of real estate or inventory management or planogramming. They remember the days of being merchants. They remember the excitement of satisfying their customers.

Yes, they have learned from and embraced new technology, using it to better manage their business. But most importantly they have used it to communicate with and better service their customers and they have never forgotten what it is to be a customer themselves.

They recognize the level of competition is such that to gain and hold onto customers, they must allow them to shop anyway they want to—the old 1,000 pound gorilla joke—whether it's on-line from their computer, over the phone, via catalog—or in-store.

Feeling a little overwhelmed? A little stressed out? Has all this vision-thing, this look to the future, given you hives? Well, that's *trend number nine*. In spite of casual clothes, working from home and entertaining shopping, the 21st century is still a stressful place.

So "kinder, gentler, more spiritual pursuits" have become essential to managing day-to-day life. Relaxing, other worldly alternatives such as yoga, meditation, herbal remedies, aromatherapy, reflexology, religion, have grown to counter the fast-paced call of life.

So as we sit in our home offices, we women "captains of industry," having finished a meeting with the production manager at our factory in Indonesia; as we modem our shopping list to husbands on their way to pick up the kids from school, we may need to kick off our sneakers, light a candle and chant the little mantra we learned at meditation class on the internet.

Speculation? Everything I've talked about today exists now—in real time in 1995. By the time we say "good morning" to Hal in 2001 the consumer landscape will have evolved even further and faster.

The key to all this is no different now that it was at the beginning of this century or at any other key benchmarks of time. The key is to continually satisfy the needs of the consumer.

Whether we call it a "paradigm shift" or "the information superhighway," in the end, if it doesn't make the consumers' life easier or better it won't last.

That may sound simplistic but it's the only truism I know that's actually true. If you haven't taken into consideration all—or even some—of the trends I mentioned today and the impact they will have on your business then get out of your office and away from printouts and talk to your kids and your parents and spouses—and your customers.

Then you too will realize it's 2001. If you're moving in the right direction all you'll see of Hal is his reflection in your rear vision mirror as you speed off down the retailing superhighway into the future. □

Index